P9-CND-462

AUDUBON HOUSE

Building the Environmentally Responsible, Energy-Efficient Office

The Wiley Series in Sustainable Design

The Wiley Series in Sustainable Design has been created for professionals responsible for, and individuals interested in, the design and construction of the built environment. The series is dedicated to the advancement of knowledge in design and construction that serves to sustain the natural environment. Titles in the series cover innovative and emerging topics related to the design and development of the human community, within the context of preserving and enhancing the quality of the natural world. Consistent with their content, books in the series are produced with care taken in the selection of recycled and non-polluting materials.

Gray World, Green Heart
Technology, Nature and the Sustainable Landscape
Robert L. Thayer, University of California, Davis

Regenerative Design for Sustainable Development
John T. Lyle, California State Polytechnic University, Pomona

Audubon House
Building the Environmentally Responsible, Energy-Efficient Office
National Audubon Society
Croxton Collaborative, Architects

AUDUBON HOUSE

Building the Environmentally Responsible, Energy-Efficient Office

National Audubon Society
Croxton Collaborative, Architects

John Wiley & Sons, Inc.
New York • Chichester • Brisbane • Toronto • Singapore

Gas Research Institute (GRI) makes no warranty or representation, express or implied, with respect to the accuracy, completeness, or usefulness of the information or the products referenced on these pages, nor that the use of any information, apparatus, method, product, or process referenced in this publication may not infringe privately owned rights. GRI assumes no liability with respect to the use of, or for damages resulting from the use of, any information, apparatus, method, product, or process referenced herein. Any warranty or representation made by the vendors of the products referenced in this publication shall be the sole responsibility of the vendors.

50%
Total Recycled Paper
10% Post-Consumer Fiber

Jacket, cover, and text manufactured using recycled materials.
This text is printed on acid-free paper.

Copyright © 1994 by National Audubon Society

All rights reserved. Published simultaneously in Canada.

Reproduction or translation of any part of this work beyond that permitted by Section 107 or 108 of the 1976 United States Copyright Act without the permission of the copyright owner is unlawful. Requests for permission or further information should be addressed to the Permissions Department, John Wiley & Sons, Inc., 605 Third Avenue, New York, NY 10158-0012.

This publication is designed to provide accurate and authoritative information in regard to the subject matter covered. It is sold with the understanding that the publisher is not engaged in rendering legal, accounting, or other professional services. If legal advice or other expert assistance is required, the services of a competent professional person should be sought.

Library of Congress Cataloging in Publication Data:
Audubon House : building the environmentally responsible, energy-efficient offices / National Audubon Society, Croxton Collaborative, architects.
    p.   cm.—(Wiley series in sustainable design)
  Includes index.
  ISBN 0-471-02496-1 (cloth : acid-free paper)
  1. Office buildings—Energy conservation. 2. Office buildings—Environmental engineering. 3. National Audubon Society—Buildings.
I. National Audubon Society. II. Croxton Collaborative (Firm)
III. Series.
TJ163.5.O35A93   1994
.696—dc20   93-46161

Printed in the United States of America

10 9 8 7 6 5 4 3 2 1

Contributors

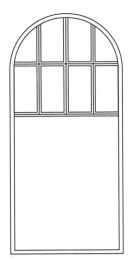

Principal Contributors to This Book

for the National Audubon Society:
Victoria Shaw, editorial director
Fred Baumgarten, editor
Mercedes Lee, writer
Lisa Yvette Waller, researcher
Jan Beyea, Ph.D., chief scientist

for Croxton Collaborative, Architects:
Randolph R. Croxton, AIA, director of architecture
Kirsten Childs, ASID, director of interior design

Audubon House Project Team Leaders

for the National Audubon Society:
Peter A. A. Berle, president and CEO
James A. Cunningham, senior vice-president for
    finance and administration
Jan Beyea, Ph.D., chief scientist

for Croxton Collaborative, architects:
Randolph R. Croxton, AIA, director of architecture
Kirsten Childs, ASID, director of interior design

Additional Team Members:

for Flack + Kurtz, consulting engineers
  Peter Flack, managing partner
  Jordan Fox, project manager and HVAC engineer
  Tom Sardo, electrical engineer
  Michael Aurelio, hydraulics and fire protection
    engineer
  Marty Salzberg, lighting designer
  Karen Goldstick, lighting designer

exterior restoration consultant
  Raymond Pepi, president, Building Conservation Associates, Inc.

structural engineer
  Robert Silman, Robert Silman Associates, P.C.
  Edward Stanley, Associate

owner's representative
  Arnold Richter, vice-president, Lehrer McGovern Bovis

contractor
  AJ Contracting, New York, N.Y. (Jerome A. Gannon, president)

Contents

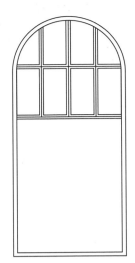

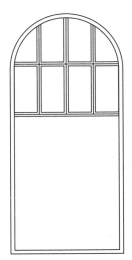

Foreword

BY PETER A. A. BERLE
President & CEO, National Audubon Society

When the National Audubon Society began its search for a new home in the early days of 1988, we had only a vague notion of what an environmentally responsible office building could be. And we could scarcely imagine the enormous impact that creating such an office would have. In the year since Audubon has occupied its new headquarters at 700 Broadway in lower Manhattan, Audubon House has been featured on network television, in *Time* and *Newsweek,* the *New York Times* and the *New Yorker,* and in nearly every architecture and interior design publication. It has drawn visitors from every corner of the globe, hundreds of whom have toured the building asking perceptive questions. In a very real sense, Audubon House has spurred a new worldwide interest in "green" architecture.

We could not ask for a better outcome. The dedicated work of the team of professionals who saw this project through to completion acquires significance in direct proportion to the number of corporate CEOs, public-sector facility managers, planners, developers, architects, interior designers, and others who take the ideas embodied in Audubon House and incorporate them into their work. While Audubon House itself makes but a small contribution to mitigating the environmental impacts of building, hundreds of thousands of buildings renovated or constructed along the same lines could make an indelible difference in the economy and the environment— saving millions of dollars of energy costs, reducing the need to exploit new sources of energy, recycling valuable natural resources and thus alleviating the growing solid waste crisis, and creating healthy, productive workplaces.

It is particularly in the economic benefits that the redesign of Audubon House stands out. As the CEO of a nonprofit organization, I understand only too well the importance of watching the bottom line. For Audubon, money saved means more money for protecting wildlife, studying and restoring ecosystems, and campaigning for a better environment. So the fact that the renovation of Audubon House could be achieved within a reasonable cost and that its energy-saving design reduces operating costs by nearly $100,000 a year gives Audubon an enormous "competitive" advantage that is passed directly to our environmental work.

I personally appeal to the CEOs of both profit and nonprofit corporations in America and around the world to consider this competitive advantage when building decisions come up. Figuring the environmental aspects of building into such decisions makes eminent fiscal sense. That is what we have learned from the Audubon experience. Being "green" is also an increasingly compelling way to sell one's business or services to a public that is ever more concerned about environmental issues. Doing business the environmental way is no longer the wave of the future: It has arrived.

The creation of environmentally responsible offices is a natural expression of the National Audubon Society's environmental goals and deep environmental commitment. Audubon's work focuses on the protection and restoration of vital habitats for wildlife and the promotion of sustainable development to ensure a healthy environment for people as well as wildlife. We believe that taking a broad "ecosystem" approach is essential. This approach aims to preserve the natural world while recognizing that human beings shape and are shaped by it. In ecosystems as diverse as the Florida Everglades, the Pacific Northwest, and the Great Lakes, Audubon has sought to find a balance that preserves the natural biological richness of these systems while taking into account the role of humankind.

Audubon also has a strong commitment to the principle of environmental justice. For too long, the conservation movement has bypassed the concerns of urban communities, the working class, the poor, and people of color. We view the urban environment and its inhabitants as having the same rights to environmental protection as do their suburban and rural counterparts. That is why Audubon's conscious choice to remain in New York City takes on such significance. We are proud to be a part of this vital urban center at the same time that we are showing that an urban office building can leave a smaller footprint than is typically believed.

Audubon House takes a big step on the path toward sustainable development. The project team left no stone unturned in looking for ways to "green" the building. Even the choice of wood furniture was carefully considered; we used only rainforest wood that had been grown sustainably, demonstrating the importance of sustainable use of resources. The recycling program at Audubon House illustrates another facet of sustainability—reducing our load on the waste stream and curtailing the waste of resources. What other office building boasts plantings on its rooftop that will feature compost made on-site?

I take enormous satisfaction in coming to work every day in a place that is comfortable and attractive to look at, where the air is fresh and the interior full of natural light. I delight in presiding over a staff that is rejuvenated by their physical workspace instead of repelled by it. And I feel great pride in knowing that Audubon House is truly an environmentally responsible edifice.

Read and enjoy this account of how Audubon House was conceived and executed, and take its message with you wherever you go.

Foreword

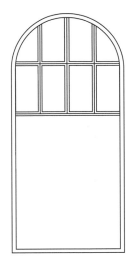

RANDOLPH R. CROXTON, AIA
Croxton Collaborative, Architects

Many people have commented that having Audubon as a client must make it relatively easy to sell an "environmental" approach. Their next observation is almost always. "Sure this makes sense for Audubon, but what about a client who doesn't have the environment as their central mission?"

We always felt that the answer to this question would be central to the long-term success of the project. Building on an approach originated with the Natural Resources Defense Council Headquarters in 1988, we constantly "tested" our decisions against the realities of the marketplace and stayed focused on value for every dollar spent. We knew that at the core of every strong environmental concept, there is an economy: the ability to "do more with less." However, to address real-world applications, we focused on demonstrated reliability and on market availability for all the basic technologies employed. Other avenues, not requiring ground-breaking technologies, led to the massive improvements in building and environmental performance that you will find described herein.

Our first advantage in this undertaking grows out of

the unbelievably poor level of energy efficiency, comfort, and indoor air quality that characterizes buildings as they are typically designed, constructed, and maintained. We see the symptoms every day in the expanding number of complaints and lawsuits by workers for poor indoor air quality, repetitive stress injury, high glare/ high stress lighted environments, and hazardous materials or practices in the workplace. Even more visible are the numerous personal fans and portable heaters people bring to work, expending even more energy trying to overcome the failure of the building to maintain comfort. Building management, as well, is often engaged in an endless attempt to balance the air-conditioning system as the sun's rays bear down on the east, south, and then west faces of the building each day.

A more intangible, but equally powerful failing is the isolation of most of a building's population from any sense of orientation, view to the outside, sense of time of day, change of season, or change of weather. Typical office design seems to approach the workplace as somewhere we "visit," a place where visual interest can be imparted through the design of the interior in isolation from the outside, as might be appropriate for some restaurants or the design of a theater. The workplace, however, is where we "live our lives," or at least the major portion of them. Therefore, there is a fundamental need to be "grounded" in the natural course of sun, weather, and season.

The possibility that design strategies to enhance these "internal" dimensions of the building could be fully integrated with the "external" or global environmental strategies addressing resource conservation, ozone depletion, acid rain, and so on, seemed somewhat remote but very challenging when we started down this road in 1988. We have since articulated these various goals as being the object of a "value-driven" design process: the three dimensions of that value being the sustainable, environmental, and humanistic dimensions.

At this point, six years later, it is clear that measurable, quantifiable improvements in the productive capacity of the atmosphere, water system, basic resources, utility grid, sanitation system, transportation system, solid waste management system, building mechanical and electrical systems, indoor air quality, lighted environment, and above all, the health, well-being, and productive capacity of people can be implemented through a comprehensive reconsideration of the process of design. Although none of us present Audubon House as an example of perfection, you will see in this case study a framework within which deeper levels of quality, performance, and value can be pursued.

If one word could summarize the approach used on Audubon House, it would be "optimization." If one word could summarize the lost opportunities in how we typically build, it would be "compliance." Buildings are increasingly delivered as products: "fast and cheap with a pretty face." Developers, construction managers, and owners will sometimes brag that their building "meets every code." In fact, if that is all they do, it is a confession. A more appropriate statement would be: "If I built this building any worse, it would be against the law."

Within Audubon House there are enhanced levels of energy efficiency, indoor air quality, pollution avoidance, CFC avoidance, solid waste management, water conservation, visual comfort, light quality, thermal comfort, and an enhanced awareness of time of day and season, and of orientation, which are achieved within an overall market rate budget for a building of this type on this site.

In Audubon House a new pattern of priorities in the investment of budget dollars is at work (no marble lobbies, rare wood paneling, or bronze handrails). Money is invested in people—in their comfort and well-being—and the payback will be in greatly enhanced productivity, due to reduced absenteeism and workplace-related illness, and the elimination of the environmental barriers to the task at hand.

Audubon House poses a challenge to our current public policy at the city, state, and national level. Clearly, there are achievable levels of massive enhancement in the way we build and renovate buildings. The question remains: When are we going to redirect the priorities and incentives of public policy to reap these rewards?

Preface

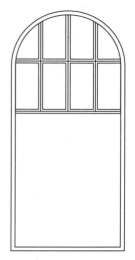

V*ision,* a term frequently overused, nonetheless may be the single word that best sums up the subject of this book: the remodeling and redesign of a century-old building to become the new headquarters of the National Audubon Society. The vision that guided this undertaking is all about seeing the act of building in a new way—thinking about its ramifications on the environment, looking for alternatives to traditional methodologies, and reconciling those objectives with the practical, business-oriented goal of economy. The result of this vision is Audubon House, a model of energy-efficient and environmentally sound building achieved at a market-rate cost.

The vision for Audubon House did not spring to life fully formed. It evolved gradually from the National Audubon Society's need to relocate to new offices in New York City and from the progressive thinking of its leaders, especially Peter Berle, who saw a singular opportunity to meld this necessity with the environmental mission of the organization. It also developed over the course of many years in the thinking and work of Randolph Croxton and Kirsten Childs, co-directors of Croxton Collaborative, Architects. Before Audubon House was ever conceived, Croxton Collaborative had already established itself among the most forward-looking architectural firms in the world.

The joining of Audubon and Croxton Collaborative in the inception of Audubon House produced that rare kind of synergy from which new ideas flow. Indeed, the collaborative process is at the very heart of the project, and that teamwork constantly shaped and reshaped the original vision even as work on Audubon House proceeded. More than the physical reality of Audubon House itself, the evolving process behind it constitutes the major purpose of this book. It is hoped that by understanding both the vision and process, the reader will have a framework from which to move toward the ideal of energy-efficient, environmentally sound building design.

Because the Audubon project emphasized teamwork so thoroughly, in this book the key players on this team are generally referred to collectively as the Audubon Team. This is understood to mean not only Audubon staff but also the principal architect and designer and the engineers. In those few instances where one or more people were solely responsible for a decision, that person or persons is identified.

Fittingly, this book was also a team effort, and I would like to extend my appreciation and thanks to all those who participated, including Curtis Johnson, our building manager, as well as to the editors and publisher at John Wiley & Sons who have made this book a reality.

—FB

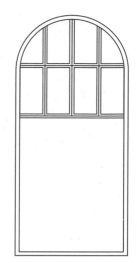

Acknowledgments

THE NATIONAL AUDUBON Society gratefully acknowledges the support of the Gas Research Institute on this project.

The National Audubon Society wishes to acknowledge the following individuals, corporations, and foundations for their generous support of our new headquarters project. By their contributions to the successful Building for an Environmental Future Campaign, these special friends have helped not only to realize a home for Audubon, but also to create a model of environmentally responsible building design. We also wish to thank the more than 15,000 Audubon members whose support of the headquarters project demonstrated their conviction that the buildings we live and work in should and can function in harmony with the natural environment.

Building for an Environmental Future Campaign

Anonymous Tradelands
Anonymous Challenge (two)
Estate of George Whittell
Members of National Audubon Society
Croxton Collaborative, Architects

The Kresge Foundation

Brooklyn Union Gas Company
Mrs. W. L. Lyons Brown, Sr.
Consolidated Edison Company of New York
Gas Research Institute
Herman Miller Inc.
Mr. and Mrs. John Phelan
Mr. and Mrs. Bayard D. Rea
Laurance S. Rockefeller

Dr. Steven C. Rockefeller
Mr. and Mrs. Phillip B. Rooney
Mr. and Mrs. Earl F. Slick
WMX Technologies, Inc.
Wheelabrator Technologies, Inc.

Mr. and Mrs. John B. Beinecke
Elizabeth Brown
Margaret W. Brown
Martin Brown
Susannah Brown
The Clark Foundation
Desso (USA) Inc.
Mr. and Mrs. Stuart S. Janney, III
Elaine Musselman
Mr. and Mrs. Robert F.
  Schumann

Anonymous
Aon Corporation
Francis H. Appleton
Audubon staff
The Vincent Astor Foundation
Mr. and Mrs. Howard P. Brokaw
A. Cary Brown
Mrs. Arnold B. Chace
Mr. and Mrs. Wallace C. Dayton
Mr. and Mrs. Noel Lee Dunn
Furniture Consultants, Inc.
The Glidden Company
The Horace W. Goldsmith Foun-
  dation
Mr. and Mrs. Edward H. Harte
Mr. and Mrs. Peter Manigault
Merrill Lynch & Co. Foundation
J. P. Morgan & Co., Inc.
Family of Laura Hadley Moseley,
  In memoriam
The New York Times Company
  Foundation, Inc.
Mr. and Mrs. Donal C. O'Brien,
  Jr.
DeWitt Peterkin
Mr. and Mrs. Samuel A. Plum
Mr. and Mrs. William Riley
Mr. and Mrs. William D. Ross
Mr. and Mrs. Harold E. Wood-
  sum, Jr.

York International

Mr. and Mrs. Leonard Block
Catherine Stewart Brown
Mr. and Mrs. Gaylord Donnelley
Mr. and Mrs. Carl Navarre, Jr.
Arthur O. Sulzberger
Ruth Test
Mr. and Mrs. Jacque D. Vallier
James T. Wallis

Dr. and Mrs. Leigh J. Altadonna
Anchorage Audubon Society
Mr. and Mrs. James Anderson
Anonymous
Mr. and Mrs. John C. Bierwirth
Mr. and Mrs. Harold Browne
Mr. and Mrs. James E. Burch
Mr. and Mrs. David C. Carson
Winthrop M. Crane, III
Dr. and Mrs. Paul R. Ehrlich
Dr. and Mrs. George Ellman
Mr. and Mrs. Charles G. Evans
Mr. and Mrs. Robert Y. Grant
Mr. and Mrs. James G. Hanes, III
Mr. and Mrs. Bruce S. Howard
Kohn Pedersen Fox Conway As-
  sociates, Inc.
The Honorable Madeleine M.
  Kunin
Last Chance Audubon Society
Mr. and Mrs. Donald R. Marble
Jan Marsh
Sara B. Musselman
Dr. and Mrs. J. P. Myers
New York City Audubon Society
Mr. and Mrs. Scott W. Reed
Robert Rowan
Leah G. Schad
Monique Schoen
Mr. and Mrs. Leonard A. Shelton
Mr. and Mrs. Peter D. Stent
Dr. and Mrs. Milton W. Weller
Mr. and Mrs. John C. Whitaker
Joan and Willard Wolfe

The Audubon Team: Key Players

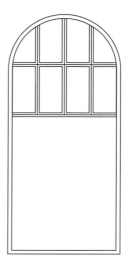

Peter A. A. Berle has been president and CEO of the National Audubon Society since 1985. Berle, an attorney, came to Audubon from Berle, Kass, and Case, a law firm he founded in 1971 that focuses primarily on environmental litigation. From 1976 to 1979 Berle was commissioner of the New York State Department of Environmental Conservation. Earlier, he served three terms in the New York State Assembly. Under Berle's leadership, Audubon has organized numerous national campaigns to protect key ecosystems such as the Arctic National Wildlife Refuge, ancient forests, wetlands, the Platte River, and the Everglades, and the society's annual operating budget has grown from $25 million to more than $45 million. Berle counts the renovation of Audubon House among his significant accomplishments. A graduate of Harvard University and Harvard Law School, Berle and his wife, Lila, have a working farm in Massachusetts. Berle enjoys cross-country skiing, running, canoeing, hiking, and fly-fishing.

James A. Cunningham is senior vice-president for finance and administration for the National Audubon Society. He has been with Audubon for 14 years. Mr. Cunningham is a certified public accountant in New York State. Working with Julian Studley & Co., Cunningham conducted the search that led to the "discovery" of the new Audubon headquarters, and he developed and executed the tax-exempt financing plan for the purchase and renovation of the building. Cunningham has a B.B.A. in business from Iona College in New Rochelle, New York, and a diploma in publishing from the New York University School of Continuing Education.

Jan Beyea, Ph.D., chief scientist for the National Audubon Society, was the lead environmental consultant on the project. He played a major role in the design and implementation of the recycling system, studied alternatives for energy systems, and analyzed data on building materials. With Audubon since 1980, Beyea has specialized in energy and solid waste issues. He serves on the EPA's Recycling Advisory Council and the Coalition of Northeastern Governors' Source Reduction Council. He is a member of the Energy Engineering Board on the National Research Council and has advised the Department of Energy on numerous energy studies. Beyea earned his doctorate in physics from Columbia University in 1970 and did research on buildings at Princeton University's Center for Energy and Environmental Studies from 1976 through 1980.

Randolph R. Croxton, AIA (American Institute of Architects), director of Architecture and Planning for Croxton Collaborative, Architects, was the chief architect for Audubon House. As such, he was responsible for coordinating the team of architects, engineering consultants, and lighting designers. He founded Croxton Collaborative in 1978 and is a nationally and internationally recognized leader in the area of environmental and sustainable building design. Besides Audubon, his many clients have included the Natural Resources Defense Council, Home Box Office, and the Riverside South Development Corporation, all in New York, and VeriFone of Costa Mesa, California. Croxton is currently a board member of the American Institute of Architects and chairman of the AIA/ACSA Research Council. He represented the AIA at the 1992 U.N. Conference on Environment and Development. Croxton received his architectural degree from North Carolina State University in 1968.

Kirsten Childs, ASID (American Society of Interior Designers), is director of Interior Design for Croxton Collaborative. Childs came to Croxton Collaborative in 1985 from the Ehrenkrantz Group, where she established a full-service Interiors Department. Childs' presence at Croxton has enabled the firm to undertake a variety of projects with a multidisciplinary approach covering every aspect of architecture, interior design, and corporate planning. Her work on the NRDC project helped earn it the first *Interiors Magazine* award for socially conscious design (1990) and the AIA national award for environmentally sensitive design in 1991. Childs' work has appeared in dozens of professional and consumer publications. She is a graduate of the Edinburgh (Scotland) College of Art and Architecture.

Peter Flack, P.E., founder and principal of Flack + Kurtz Consulting Engineers, oversaw the Audubon project's engineering design. He is a recognized expert in the design of energy-efficient, cost-effective buildings and as head of the firm for more than 25 years has turned the company into a leader in the field. Besides Audubon House, Flack's past work includes the NRDC headquarters and the World Financial Center in New York, and Disney Corporate Headquarters in California. He received a B.S.M.E. in mechanical engineering from New York University in 1951 and is a licensed professional engineer in many states. His current activities include the American Business Center at Checkpoint Charlie in Berlin and the new Museum of Modern Art in San Francisco.

Jordan Fox is also a principal of Flack + Kurtz Consulting Engineers specializing in mechanical engineering. His experience includes corporate offices, financial institutions, transportation facilities, retail stores and malls, and more. For the Audubon project he functioned as project manager and HVAC engineer, managing the day-to-day engineering aspects of the project. Fox has a B.S.M.E. in mechanical engineering from the University of Rhode Island.

Marty Salzberg, project manager, Flack + Kurtz Consulting Engineers, specializes in lighting design and was the chief lighting designer for Audubon House. She joined Flack + Kurtz in 1989 with five years of lighting design experience in New York. Her projects with the firm have included the Sony USA headquarters in New York, the USTA National Tennis Center at Flushing Meadow, Queens, and the Dibner Library of Polytechnic University in Brooklyn. Salzberg studied at the Parsons School of Design in New York and has a bachelor's degree from Brandeis University in Massachusetts. She is a member of the International Association of Lighting Designers.

Thomas Sardo, associate, Flack + Kurtz Consulting Engineers, specializes in electrical and fire life safety systems design. He is responsible for the design and development of electrical documents and construction supervision of both base building and tenant electrical work. His experience includes One and Two Independence Square, Washington, D.C., IBM Credit Corporation, Stamford, Connecticut, Mellon Bank Center in Philadelphia, and Barney's and NRDC in New York City. Sardo has a B.E.E. in electrical engineering from Cooper Union, New York.

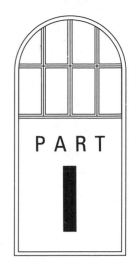

PART

I

TOWARD A SUSTAINABLE ARCHITECTURE

Principles and Process

Audubon House, headquarters of the National Audubon Society, at 700 Broadway in New York City; a schematic sketch of the south and west exterior elevations. Built in 1891 by George W. Post, this classic eight-story pre-skyscraper building was renovated in 1991–1992 as a model of environmentally sound and energy-efficient design. (Courtesy of Croxton Collaborative, Architects.)

Introduction

FOR MOST PEOPLE, the last image that comes to mind when they think of a large environmental group—especially one with an affinity for wildlife—is that of an office building in New York City. Yet that is exactly what this book is about. And this book is written in the hope that more people will start thinking about office buildings when they think about the environment.

Between 1989 and 1992, the National Audubon Society (Audubon) purchased and renovated a century-old building in lower Manahattan that became the society's new headquarters. Located at 700 Broadway, in a lively district that features the campus of New York University, Audubon House is an eight-story building (a ninth-floor conference center was added during the renovation) with a little less than 100,000 square feet of space. The fourth through eighth floors house Audubon's headquarters staff of about 170 full-time employees. The first floor is given over to retail space and the second and third floors will be leased to other nonprofit organizations until Audubon needs room to expand.

The building itself is a fine example of early twentieth-century urban architecture, with a beautiful multihued exterior, but the story of Audubon House really begins inside. Under the direction of the architectural firm of Croxton Collaborative, the building's interior was not just renovated but remodeled. Working together with a common purpose, the architects, engineers, and Audubon (the "Audubon Team") designed a building that attains high standards of energy efficiency and environmental performance (reduced impact on the natural environment), as well as high indoor air quality—all at "market rate" for a comparable renovation project.

To conserve and restore natural ecosystems, focusing on birds and other wildlife for the benefit of humanity and the earth's biological diversity.
NATIONAL AUDUBON SOCIETY MISSION

Why Audubon? And why an office building in New York City? To answer these questions, we must first examine the context in which Audubon operates. What are the national and global issues facing Audubon—an internationally known environmental group of about 500,000 members spread over 50 states and several countries—and, more important, facing everyone?

In 1992, the leaders of more than 150 nations and representatives from environmental groups worldwide (including Audubon and Croxton) met in Rio de Janeiro for the U.N. Conference on Environment and Development, or "Earth Summit." Besides being the first international meeting of its kind to focus on the interface between environmental and development issues, the Earth Summit addressed a range of pressing global environmental concerns, among them atmospheric change and the effects of pollution, resource depletion, habitat loss, and the rapid extinction of species. Not inconsequentially, each of these has profound effects on human survival and quality of life.

Atmospheric change, or global warming, is a disturbing long-range environmental trend of the twentieth century and a leading concern among American citizens. While there remains some dispute over the magnitude of global warming and whether the ominous rise in temperatures during the last decade "proves" its existence, almost no one disputes the fact that carbon dioxide and other "greenhouse gases" trap heat, causing the earth's temperature to increase. Nor can it be disputed that human industry continues to pump ever-increasing concentrations of greenhouse gases into the atmosphere. According to the Worldwatch Institute, atmospheric concentrations of carbon dioxide rose 13 percent between 1959 and 1992, and if current rates continue, worldwide temperatures could rise between 1.5 and 4.5 degrees Celsius by the late twenty-first century.[1]

Scientists agree that the consequences of global warming could be disastrous, including rising sea levels that would flood low-lying regions, greater extremes in weather fluctuations accompanied by more intense weather events such as storms and droughts, and widespread extinctions as the climate changes.[2] All the nations attending the Earth Summit have now signed a declaration to reduce worldwide production of greenhouse gases and to combat global warming.

Another type of atmospheric change that has been well established is the depletion of the stratospheric ozone layer. This layer helps protect the earth from harmful doses of solar ultraviolet radiation, but it has been thinned over many regions primarily by the introduction of human-made gases into the atmosphere, the most lethal of which are chlorofluorocarbons (CFCs). Although an international agreement signed in 1987 calls for phasing out production of CFCs by the year 2000, the effects of ozone depletion are expected to last well into the next century.

Air pollution takes many forms: high levels of ozone in the lower atmosphere choke many urban areas, combining with dust and other pollutants to create smog. Acid rain is caused by emissions of sulfur dioxides and nitrogen oxides from the burning of fossil fuels. It is of particular concern in the Northeast, where acid rain from coal-burning plants in the Midwest is thought to have acidified and killed mountain lakes in the Adirondacks and

---

[1] Lester R. Brown et al., *Vital Signs 1993: The Trends That Are Shaping Our Future* (New York: W. W. Norton, 1993).
[2] *Audubon Activist* (Jan. 1991).

elsewhere. Increasing attention is also being paid to the local effects of incinerators and chemical factories that emit toxic fumes.

The depletion of natural resources has accelerated in recent years. For example, Japan has already cut so much of its forests that it must import most of its wood. Similarly, the United States now imports more than half of its oil because domestic oil reserves, once though limitless, are being depleted. In many areas of the world, particularly in the developing countries, once-fertile soils have been turned to desert by overuse, contributing to famine.

Habitat loss and loss of biodiversity, the handmaidens of natural resource depletion, have simultaneously reached alarming proportions. Most educated people are now aware of the importance of the tropical rainforests as well as their rapid destruction, yet the devastation continues at the rate of about 1 percent a year.[3] In the United States, too, vital habitat and species are fast disappearing. At least 300,000 acres of wetlands, for example, are lost each year, and more than 4,000 species of plants and animals are on, or are candidates for, the endangered species list.

The question remains, however: What does all this have to do with an office building? The answer can be found in the enormous impact that buildings have on the environment. To take just one example, the "built environment"—the aggregate of all buildings and the structures that support them—is estimated to account for more than half of primary energy use in the United States.[4] Office buildings alone account more than a quarter of the peak electricity demand in the United States.[5] Peak demand is the chief catalyst for new energy development. These factors alone have ramifications for climate change, resource depletion, pollution, and habitat

[3] World Resources Institute, *World Resources 1992–1993* (New York: Oxford University Press, 1992).
[4] See the diagram on page 26 and the accompanying discussion for a fuller explanation of this figure.
[5] *Monthly Energy Review* (June 1992). Department of Energy/Energy Information Administration, Washington, D.C.

and biodiversity loss—in short, for the whole range of environmental problems. In Chapter 2 we look in more detail at the impact of office buildings and the built environment.

At the Earth Summit, world leaders and environmental activists alike put forth the concept of *sustainable development* as a broad-based solution to the growing litany of environmental problems. Sustainable development is characterized by the use of resources to create an acceptable standard of living *but in a way that ensures the viability of future generations.* If we accept that sustainable development provides a way out of our environmental dilemma, then building owners, archi-

Lever House, New York City. Built in 1954, Lever House was among the first Modern-style office buildings, employing the post–World War II glass-wall technology. By the time of the office building boom of the late 1970s and 1980s, however, such considered design had already been largely replaced by time- and first-cost-driven "pre-packaged" designs. (Courtesy of Unilever United States, Inc.)

tects, and others in the building profession must begin to ask: Is there an equivalent *sustainable architecture*—one that through energy efficiency and the frugal use of natural resources helps ensure the viability of future generations? Not long ago, Audubon got the opportunity to answer that question.

Time to Move

In 1987, Audubon initiated a search for a new location for its national headquarters. At the time, Audubon was leasing four floors (plus some additional storage space in the basement) of a 30-story skyscraper in midtown Manhattan. In 1971, when the society moved in, it was paying $244,162 for 29,733 square feet of space in the then-new building, or $8.21 per square foot. By 1987, the rent was skyrocketing by more than $100,000 a year, and by the time Audubon would leave the building, in 1992, it would be paying more than a $1,000,000 a year for 40,000 square feet, or more than $30 per square foot. Given these rising costs, Audubon urgently needed to find an alternative that would cost less, save more money for environmental programs, and allow the organization room to grow.

We hope that Audubon House is not seen as an isolated example of a building created by environmentalists but as a vehicle for real change in the way building is practiced worldwide.
PETER A. A. BERLE, PRESIDENT OF THE
NATIONAL AUDUBON SOCIETY

While financial necessity was the primary reason for Audubon's decision to move, high rents were not the only problem with Audubon's then-headquarters. The midtown office tower embodied many of the worst traits of glass-box construction—not the least of which was its (to many people) unattractive appearance. The exterior consisted of a sheath of glass overlaid on a spine of concrete. Indoors, a glittery lobby gave way to floor after floor of nearly identical, featureless offices, enclosed by tinted, permanently shut windows.

The air inside the offices was notoriously stuffy. In summer, Audubon employees needed a barrage of fans to circulate the air; in winter, open areas could be overly warm while perimeter offices often required portable electric heaters to supplement the building's heating system. Hallways as well as offices were lit by rows of "cold" fluorescent lights recessed into the ceiling and enclosed by frosted plastic lenses. Employees frequently complained of headache, fatigue, foul odors, and respiratory discomforts.

By 1988, the search for a new Audubon home, led by Audubon President Peter A. A. Berle and Chief Financial

Audubon House, exterior facing Broadway, prior to renovation. Except for the ground level, the building was unoccupied when Audubon purchased it in 1989, yet the exterior was in remarkably good condition. Under the direction of the architectural firm Croxton Collaborative, the decayed interior was demolished and renovated according to environmental precepts. (Courtesy of Bernstein Associates.)

Officer James Cunningham, began in earnest. Building ownership quickly emerged as the best option; given market conditions in New York, the savings on rent would more than compensate for the cost of purchasing a building or even of new construction. As a nonprofit organization, Audubon also had the advantage of being eligible for tax-exempt financing. The search culminated in 1989 with the purchase of the eight-story former Schermerhorn Building at 700 Broadway in lower Manhattan, at a cost of $10 million. (A four-year capital cam-

Exterior, showing detail of window arches. Post's sophisticated design, articulating the building in three sections, was based on popular models of the day, including Richardson's Marshall Field store in Chicago. A multitextured and multihued effect is achieved with a mixture of brownstone, masonry, and terra-cotta. This and the twisted columns and carved stonework are characteristic of the Romanesque Revival style. (Photo by Tom Mead.)

paign subsequently grossed more than $14 million, to help offset the cost of purchase and renovation.)

Formerly named for the New York merchant family that commissioned it, the building was completed in 1891 and is an outstanding example of late nineteenth century Romanesque Revival architecture. Its architect was George W. Post, a leading practitioner of the day whose oeuvre includes the New York Stock Exchange, a Neoclassical masterpiece, and the Williamsburg Bank in Brooklyn.

Exterior, detail showing capital on window pilaster. The elaborate carved stonework of Audubon House has survived mostly intact, including the carved series of grotesque faces along the building's cornice—allegedly caricatures of leading public figures of the time. (Photo by Otto Baitz.)

The Audubon building employs a cast-iron frame supported by load-bearing walls and below-ground masonry pillars. The exterior consists of glazed masonry brick, brownstone, and terra-cotta, creating a multihued and multitextured effect. The facade is classically separated into three segments: a solid two-story base; the middle four stories, distinguished by sweeping arches; and the top two stories, featuring smaller double arches. Following the popular style of the time, a number of Romanesque revival details enliven the building, and a series of carved grotesque human faces runs along the cornice.

Except for retail establishments on the ground floor, the building had been vacant for more than 10 years when Audubon bought it. Despite the building's age, it was structurally sound; the exterior was in remarkably good condition, while the interior needed extensive renovation. With 98,000 square feet of space, the building was more than adequate for the Audubon Society to grow. It was also conveniently near mass transit (subways), in a vibrant neighborhood adjacent to the New York University campus and Soho, a lively area of art galleries and retail stores.

Audubon had found its "dream house." But already the Audubon leadership was undergoing a major transformation in thinking about the impending renovation. What was the proper role for an environmental organization within its own "environment"? What were the environmental impacts of renovating and occupying a building? Could these be significantly reduced at Audubon, and by extension, by others? Could a building be used to further Audubon's environmental mission?

Some saw in this last question a built-in contradiction, believing that the goal of preserving and restoring nature could never be reconciled with the task of renovating a modern, urban office building. Audubon's leaders believed otherwise. They envisioned a building that would exist in harmony with its environment and that, by saving energy and resources, would point the way to saving whole ecosystems. Fortunately, they did not have to go far to find a precedent.

Natural Resources Defense Council, New York City, main stairway and reception area. In 1988, Croxton Collaborative redesigned the NRDC headquarters, cutting electricity consumption by more than half and installing low-toxic materials. On the basis of that work, the National Audubon Society selected Croxton Collaborative to redesign its new headquarters at 700 Broadway. (Photo by Otto Baitz.)

In 1988, Croxton Collaborative, under the leadership of co-directors Randolph Croxton and Kirsten Childs, completed the redesign and renovation of the offices of the Natural Resources Defense Council (NRDC), another New York–based environmental group, which occupied three floors of a lower Manhattan loft. The NRDC redesign was a signal achievement for the firm, combining energy efficiency and environmental performance largely through design modifications, while creating a strikingly healthy workplace through new approaches to materials and systems design criteria.

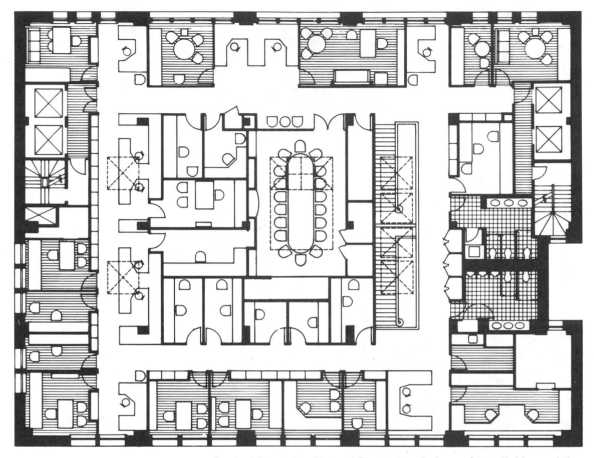

Typical floor plan, Natural Resources Defense Council. Many of the methods used at NRDC were adapted or built upon at Audubon House, such as the "daylighting" of the interior with open plans and the installation of clerestory windows in the perimeter offices. (Courtesy of Croxton Collaborative, Architects.)

Not long after touring the NRDC headquarters in 1989, Berle selected Croxton Collaborative to direct the renovation of 700 Broadway, with Flack + Kurtz as engineers. What began as a need to relocate had by now evolved into a full-fledged project to apply the principle of sustainability to the renovation of an entire building. Work began in early 1990 and was completed in November 1992 at a total cost of $14 million. The new Audubon House was formally dedicated on December 3, 1992.

A Living Model

One year after its opening, Audubon House stands as a milestone of environmentally sound, energy-efficient, healthy, and humane building design—an antidote to the plague of standard-issue, grossly inefficient office buildings that dot urban and suburban landscapes. To some extent, Audubon House's significance can be measured statistically by comparing its performance to what it would have been if the redesign had been "code compliant"—that is, if it merely met the minimum legal and professional standards—or had used conventional equipment. Compared to a code-compliant building, for example, Audubon House consumes 62 percent less overall energy and delivers approximately 30 percent more outdoor air to its occupants. By using a gas-fired heating and cooling system instead of a conventional system, Audubon House eliminates emissions of sulfur oxides and CFCs entirely, and reduces emissions of nitrogen oxides an estimated 60 percent.[6]

Other benefits of Audubon House, though equally important, are more difficult to quantify. A higher rate of air exchange and the greater influx of outdoor air, combined with use of low-toxic materials throughout the building, make the indoor air noticeably "fresher." Materials made with recycled content are deployed whenever possible, reducing the demand for virgin natural resources. A built-in recycling system at Audubon House is designed to capture as much as 80 percent of normal office waste. And not incidentally, Audubon House is a comfortable, light, and pleasant environment in which to work.

Audubon's decision to move to an existing building within New York City rather than to relocate elsewhere or to construct a new building is another fundamental environmental feature of the project. Implicit in this decision are a respect for the urban environment and an acknowledgment of its increasing importance as an envi-

---

[6] Fuller explanations of these statistics can be found in relevant chapters in Part II of this book.

ronmental issue. It might have been "easy" for Audubon to leave the city for the suburbs, as so many corporations have done in recent years, especially since Audubon's constituency is at present largely suburban.[7]

This migration has taken a devastating toll on American cities, however, as well as bringing unbridled development farther and farther into the countryside. It also has further increased Americans' dependence on the least efficient form of transportation, the automobile. Anyone driving through, say, Detroit—or dozens of similar American cities—sees the effects of this urban dissolution. Freeways connect the "inner city," huge portions of which are impoverished or abandoned, to suburbs that extend for miles beyond; along the sides of the freeways sprout endless insular, glass office buildings and sprawling shopping malls.

Audubon consciously took no new, previously undeveloped land to build a new building, thus making no direct contribution to loss of habitat. By choosing to renovate an existing structure, moreover, rather than tearing it down and building a new one, Audubon not only saved resources (see Chapter 7) but also preserved an important part of New York's urban fabric—a building of great distinction and historic significance.

Of greater importance than the direct benefits of Audubon House to its occupants, local environs, and the global environment is its potential to change the practice of building and by so doing to reduce dramatically the impact that buildings everywhere have on the environment. In a very real sense, the Audubon project poses a question: What if every new building were designed with the same approach as that used by the Audubon Team?

---

[7] Several other factors influenced Audubon's decision to stay in New York City, although there was some discussion at the time about moving to Washington, D.C., where many environmental groups are based, or to suburban Westchester County, north of New York City. For one thing, New York City is the historical base of the National Audubon Society, which formed at the turn of the century largely to end the trade in bird plumes, which was centered in New York City. For another, it continues to be a productive base for Audubon's publishing and fund-raising operations. And existing staff, the majority of whom lived in the city, would not be displaced or forced to commute long distances. For more information, cf. Frank Graham, *The Audubon Ark: A History of the National Audubon Society* (New York: Alfred A. Knopf, 1990).

One estimate offers a clue: If every building in the United States reduced its direct and indirect output of CFCs to virtually zero, as Audubon did, total emissions of CFCs would instantly be cut by 25 percent.[8] Or this: If all new office and commercial buildings built between now and 2020 used the same approach, it could save an estimated 100,000 megawatts a day—the total amount presently consumed by the commercial sector—and eliminate the need for roughly 50 new nuclear power plants.[9]

A New Approach

What is this new approach? To begin with, it is decidedly not "business as usual." Instead, it challenges the prevailing assumptions and practices of building and renovation. It places environmental criteria, including the sustainable use of resources, energy efficiency, and air quality, on an equal footing with traditional criteria of cost, functionality, and aesthetics. And it makes the case that a building can reconcile all these concerns and still be comfortable for its occupants and *cost-effective*. More than any other, this last point distinguishes the Audubon Team's approach from most earlier "green" architecture.

In fact, it *is* the point: Audubon House demonstrates that *environmental performance and economic sense are compatible*. Most "green" buildings are relegated to the margins and marked as expensive prototypes. They are viewed not as real buildings with real people who have needs for comfort and productivity, and they are seen as inherently contradictory to the primary directive of business—to cut costs. Lacking any other perspective, the vast majority of owners and builders proceed from one project to the next, continuing to build with one overriding goal: to save money up front.

Audubon House disproves once and for all the old assumptions and overturns destructive priorities, replac-

---

[8] Jan Beyea et al., *Diet for a Greenhouse Planet* (New York: National Audubon Society, 1989). Based on total production of CFCs by the building sector.
[9] Natural Resources Defense Council, pers. comm.

ing them with a fundamentally new paradigm. The renovation of Audubon's headquarters was completed at a competitive market rate, and its energy-saving features *reduce* operating costs by as much as $100,000 a year over the energy costs of a comparable code-compliant building. By achieving a superior level of indoor air quality, Audubon House is expected to save the society thousands more dollars by increasing worker productivity. All together, Audubon's ownership and renovation of 700 Broadway are projected to save the society $1 million a year by 1995 compared to the amount the society would have been spending had it remained at its old address.

> *The grandeur and rich history of the urban environment are written in its architecture. Unfortunately these qualities are fast disappearing in favor of cookie-cutter skyscrapers. By choosing to renovate this building we were able to preserve a piece of New York history, as well as to achieve our environmental goals.*
>
> PETER A. A. BERLE

Besides making the timely point that environmental and economic considerations go hand in hand, Audubon House is designed to be an accessible model. To that end, it employs "holistic" or "integrated" design concepts, relying on seemingly simple, interlocking design decisions that produce cumulative energy savings and a range of environmental benefits. In addition, it uses "off-the-shelf" products and technologies that are widely available to practicing professionals.

Yet the approach used for Audubon House cannot be duplicated in whole, nor should it be. Each project must be shaped by the requirements of the participants, the particulars of the site, and other factors. The Audubon Team's approach describes a general process, in actuality a conceptual framework, that if studied and elaborated on can lead to a desirable outcome—a greener, healthier building. In addition to the new set of priorities outlined above, this process requires a different set of standards for decision making and a different yardstick for measuring results; a nontraditional approach to relationships among professionals and greater participation from owners; and, above all, an investment of time and intellectual rigor greater than is usually expected—until such time, at least, that environmental, sustainable design becomes the norm and its procedures become firmly established.

The rewards of this analytical approach are great. For architects, interior designers, engineers, and other professionals, it opens up new avenues that add value to their services and allows them to tailor decisions according to the particular needs of a project. (Architects in particular can point to the Audubon model when convincing owners of the value in environmental design.) For owners, it shines a positive light on their corporations or institutions and saves on the bottom line. As each new project advances the goals embodied at Audubon, it will cause politicians and decision makers to reevaluate the standards by which buildings are judged and the codes and regulations that guide building practices. Finally, it is hoped that the example of Audubon House and all that follow it will lead the way to a new enlightened era that will make a more livable and green planet for all.

How To Use This Book

This book is intended to be a starting point for professionals in architecture, interior design, engineering, and related professions who are interested in environmentally conscious, cost-effective building design. It describes the general approach used by the Audubon Team in renovating Audubon House, as well as some of the lessons learned in the process. This book is also for corporate executives, urban planners, government leaders, and developers—anyone who plays a part in making decisions about constructing new buildings or renovating old ones. It is hoped that you will see the value of the Audubon model as a guide to your own projects.

And this book is for the general reader, because the story of Audubon House is about working and thinking in new ways and about putting environmental values—the quality of life of our children and grandchildren—in the forefront. These issues concern everyone.

In the next two chapters, we examine in greater detail the effects of the built environment on our·environment and the principles and processes that guided the Audubon project. In the second part of this book, we take you inside Audubon House for a look at the designs, systems, and products that make it work. The third and final part of this book consists of technical appendices. Here architects and other professionals will find resources on building products and other technical data.

The appendices include a brief list of products used at Audubon House and their vendors; this is provided solely as a *starting point for research*. It is *not* a complete list by any means; it is *not* a substitute for careful research of one's own; and the products and vendors listed are *not* endorsed by National Audubon Society or Croxton Collaborative. Product specifications constantly change and advances happen with regularity. (The specifications for Audubon House were developed in 1991.) Homeowners looking for product information may be disappointed not to find the products used at Audubon or even equivalent items at retail home products stores. However, many of the general approaches used for the Audubon project can be adapted creatively to building, renovating, restoring, or even living in a home, and homeowners wishing to be "green" are encouraged to give it a try.

The Built Environment: Counting the Costs

2

FEW ASPECTS OF the American landscape are as ubiquitous as the office building. Shiny office towers define the skylines of our major cities, and countless office complexes line our highways all the way out to suburbia. According to one estimate, there is at least 3.2 billion square feet of rentable office space in the United States (not including owner-occupied offices).[10] Less than half (45 percent) lies within "central business districts" (i.e., downtown areas). Manhattan is the leading market for office space, with 353 million square feet.[11]

The 1970s and especially the 1980s witnessed an unprecedented boom in office construction, fueled by the speculative real-estate markets and "junk bond" financing, which resulted in "overbuilding." With the decline in the real estate market in the 1990s, the folly of overbuilding quickly became obvious as vacancy rates for office space soared; in some cities a quarter or more of the space remains vacant.[12] In New York City the vacancy rate stood at 13.7 percent in 1990. To some extent the trend toward new building has abated, but in 1990 there

---

[10] Society of Industrial and Office Realtors, *Comparative Statistics of Industrial and Office Real Estate Markets* (Washington, D.C. 1991).
[11] Ibid.
[12] Ibid.

During the office construction boom of the late 1970s and 1980s, "glass box" commercial buildings sprung up in urban and especially suburban areas. Built with little consideration for local climate or other site-specific considerations, such buildings have squandered enormous quantities of energy and created unhealthy indoor environments. Their emphasis on the automobile rather than on public transportation has further wasted the nation's energy and resources. (Photo courtesy of Trammell Crow Company, Lighton Plaza Complex, Overland Park, Kansas.)

was still nearly 3 million square feet of office space under construction in Manhattan. At the same time, occupancy was declining by more than 2 million square feet.[13]

Vacancy is but one consequence of overbuilding but perhaps the easiest to measure. Other effects are more difficult to quantify but bear directly on the environmental impacts of office buildings: habitats are destroyed to site new offices; huge quantities of natural resources are used to construct them; ever-increasing amounts of energy must be provided for them.

Overbuilding also describes the manner in which typi-

---

[13] Ibid.

cal building projects are conceived and engineered: rather than being built on a scale suited to a limited number of occupants and their needs, they are built to accommodate growing numbers of occupants—numbers that do not exist. The result is outsized office buildings. At the height of the office boom, a building was proposed for midtown Manhattan that would have cast an all-day shadow across a portion of Central Park. In the rush to build more buildings and the exodus from the cities to the suburbs, expediency has become a leading priority of architects and engineers. One can see its results in the sameness of one glass-walled office building after another. Rarely are location, climate, and other site-specific conditions taken into account. The majority of these buildings do not realize the levels of efficiency and health that can be easily attained.

Energy and Pollution

To appreciate the full impact of overbuilding on the environment, as well as the enormous opportunity that building professionals have to mitigate these impacts, one has to look not just at office buildings but at the entire *built environment,* of which offices are just a part. The built environment includes not only all buildings—residential, commercial, and industrial—but also infrastructure (roads, bridges, parking lots, etc.). Perhaps because the built environment is where most of us spend the majority of our lives, we rarely stop to consider its impact on the natural environment. Yet that impact is dramatic.

An indication of this can be seen in the diagram shown here developed by Croxton Collaborative, showing the total primary energy use by the built environment. Standard calculations partition energy consumption into four sectors: residential, commercial, industrial, and transportation (left side of diagram; numbers in squares show percentage of energy use in each sector) and stop there. This diagram goes a critical step beyond, redistributing energy consumption according to its end use (arrows go-

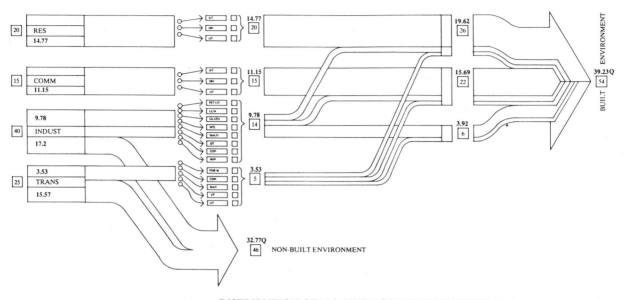

DISTRIBUTION OF U.S. PRIMARY ENERGY USE TO THE BUILT ENVIRONMENT

1982 = 72 QUADS (Statistical Distribution Above)
1990 = 81 QUADS

© Croxton Collaborative, Architects

November 1991

Distribution of U.S. primary energy use to the built environment. The U.S. Department of Energy identifies energy in four categories: residential, commercial, industrial, and transportation. To gain a better understanding of the total energy consumed by the "built environment" (all buildings and their infrastructure), Croxton Collaborative, with physicist Francesco Tubiello, undertook this analysis.

The diagram, read left to right, shows that by separating energy use in the four categories by its constituent processes, and then redistributing it according to its destination or end use, the built environment is seen to consume 54 percent of primary energy in the United States in the base year 1992. The built environment is thus the major user of energy; by the same token, building professionals have the opportunity to contribute significantly to overall energy conservation.

Numbers in squares are percentages; numbers outside squares are energy consumption in quads (1 quad = 10^{15} Btu). Key to processes: residential (res.) and commercial (comm.): SIT, site; SRC, source; OT, other. Industrial (indust.) and transportation (Trans.): PET-CH, petrochemicals; LUM, lumber; SL-STO, steel-stone; MTL, metals; MACH, machinery; CON, construction; MIN, mining; FOR-N, forestry/natural resources; CON, construction; MAN, manufacturing; OT, other. (Courtesy of Croxton Collaborative, Architects.)

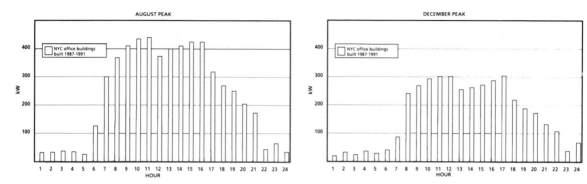

Energy use of a minimally code-compliant building, August and December. Peak demand is defined as the energy use during the period of greatest need. In New York, peak demand occurs in the dog days of August, when air conditioners are at full blast; on a daily basis, peak demand for office buildings occurs at midday. Reducing peak demand is key to energy conservation and helps eliminate the need for new sources of energy. (Courtesy of Energy Simulation Specialists.)

ing left to right). For example, more than half the primarily energy consumed by the industrial sector goes toward the built environment—some into residential buildings, some into commercial buildings, and the rest into industrial buildings (factories). Similarly, a small but nonetheless significant portion of the energy used by the transportation sector goes into construction—the built environment—in each of the other three sectors. In sum, these revised calculations project that the built environment consumes more than half—54 percent in the base year 1982—of the primary energy in the United States. Clearly, the greatest potential for reducing energy consumption lies with the built environment.[14]

Another way of understanding the significant role of buildings in consuming energy is by measuring peak demand for electricity—the amount used during the period of greatest demand. (In New York City, for example,

---

[14] The energy figures by sector is based on U.S. Department of Energy statistics for 1982; the breakdown of products and redistribution into built and nonbuilt categories is based on the same year's data from the Department of Commerce.

peak demand occurs in August, when air conditioners are at full blast.). Office buildings and workplaces alone account for more than a quarter of peak electricity demand in the United States, a figure exceeding annually the output of all existing U.S. nuclear plants.[15] These figures give little indication of changing. It is estimated that by 2020 the appetite for electricity in the commercial sector will double; if it were powered solely by nuclear energy, it would require the construction of about 40 new nuclear power plants.[16]

Traditionally, the building industry has been dominated by an approach that is minimally code-compliant. This inherently results in buildings that are the worst the law will allow. At Audubon House we focused on highest cost justifiable performance. Code minimums were left far behind.

RANDOLPH CROXTON

The insatiable demand for energy and the natural resources that produce it lies at the very heart of many of our environmental problems. Industrial nations consume the lion's share of world energy; in 1989, commercial energy consumption in industrialized countries was nearly three times greater than that of developing countries.[17] At the same time, energy production in industrialized nations has fallen off as proven reserves dry up. For instance, according to one estimate, at current rates of production the United States and Canada combined have approximately only 10 years of oil in proven reserves.[18]

While supplies are diminishing, however, demand con-

---

[15] *Monthly Energy Review* (June 1992). Department of Energy/Energy Information Administration, Washington, D.C.

[16] Approximate figures based on *Monthly Energy Review* (June 1992) and *The Future of Electric Power in America: Economic Supply for Economic Growth* Washington, D.C.: U.S. Department of Energy, Office of Policy, Planning and Analysis, June 1983).

[17] World Resources Institute, op. cit.

[18] Ibid.

tinues to increase, forcing countries like the United States to import more resources, build more questionable nuclear power plants, or prompting them to seek out remote but ecologically priceless tracts for energy development. Thus the U.S. oil industry has increasingly coveted the biologically rich Arctic National Wildlife Refuge in Alaska and vast areas of the Continental Shelf, and only the objections of environmentalists (including the National Audubon Society) and concerned citizens have thwarted it.

Closer to home for Audubon, increasing demand for electricity in the United States has caused utilities in the Northeast to consider importing hydroelectricity from Hydro-Quebec, a Canadian government–owned utility. To meet the demand, Hydro-Quebec has proposed a vast series of dams throughout Canada's James Bay region that would destroy hundreds of thousands of acres of mostly unspoiled subarctic habitat and flood the remaining traditional hunting grounds of the native Cree

James Bay region, Quebec. The provincial utility, Hydro-Quebec, plans to build an array of large hydroelectric dams around James Bay, threatening the largely unspoiled subarctic ecosystem and the livelihood of the native Cree. Some of the construction would be financed through the sale of electricity to states in the Northeastern United States, including New York. Because the Audubon Society opposes further development around James Bay, it sought to reduce the demand for electricity at Audubon House. (Photo by Steve Young.)

Dam and riverbed, James Bay region, Quebec. Contrary to a popular notion, hydroelectricity is not a benign energy source. Dams already constructed around James Bay have destroyed thousands of acres of habitat and disrupted people and wildlife. (Photo by Ted Levine.)

people. Audubon has been a major participant in opposing the James Bay projects, and during the renovation of Audubon House, the society put a major emphasis on reducing electricity consumption in order not to contribute to the problem.

In addition to problems of supply, the production and transportation of energy are fraught with difficulties as well. In the case of oil, for example, the by-products of oil drilling include toxic substances, often discarded in shallow pits, that can harm wildlife and leak into groundwater. The hazards of transporting oil are well known from such events as the *Exxon Valdez* oil spill, but it is widely believed that more oil is probably lost through small unrecorded spills and leaks than through major disasters. The production of nuclear energy and transportation and disposal of spent fuel raises serious safety questions. Even relatively clean forms of energy such as biomass (burning of plant matter) are not without problems.

Resource conservation involves a cradle-to-cradle approach to building. Audubon House offered us the opportunity to reduce significant levels of consumption and waste in the built environment.
JAN BEYEA, AUDUBON CHIEF SCIENTIST.

The most serious consequence of energy consumption, however, is the emission of pollutants into the air. The burning of fossil fuels (oil, coal, and natural gas) produces large quantities of carbon dioxide, the leading cause of global warming. The United States is easily the leading industrial producer of carbon dioxide in the world, accounting for close to a quarter (22 percent) of worldwide carbon dioxide emissions from fossil-fuel burning and cement mixing; per capita, carbon dioxide emissions in this country are also among the highest in the world—almost five times the worldwide average.[19] Annually, U.S. output of carbon dioxide is more than 5 billion tons. The commercial sector—office buildings, stores, institutions—accounts for around 740 million tons a year, or 14 percent (although, as noted above, the entire built environment is estimated to contribute more than 50 percent).[20]

Fossil-fuel burning, particularly of coal, produces sulfur oxides and nitrogen oxides, the key sources of acid rain. With the gradual moving away from coal as a leading energy source, sulfur dioxide production in the

---

[19] World Resources Institute, op. cit.
[20] Beyea et al., op. cit.

United States has declined from around 30 million tons in 1970 to 20 million tons in 1990; 70 percent of this output comes from power generation and another 4 percent directly from the commercial sector. Nitrogen oxide emissions, which are also a leading constituent of automobile exhaust, have remained steady at around 20 million tons a year, with power plants contributing roughly 37 percent and commercial establishments around 3 percent.[21]

Although not a significant by-product of fossil-fuel burning, chlorofluorocarbons (CFCs) deserve mention because they are a product of building-related activities: air conditioning and the manufacture and installation of foam insulation. CFCs have been estimated to cause up to 25 percent of the greenhouse effect that causes global warming and they are the major cause of stratospheric ozone depletion ("ozone holes"). Not surprisingly, the United States leads the world in CFC production, contributing around 23 percent.[22] About a quarter of this output has been directly and indirectly attributed to buildings (other than residences).

Embodied Energy and Natural Resources

Before its first light is ever switched on, a building will have consumed a vast quantity of energy. This energy, expended in the extraction and processing of raw materials, transportation, and construction, is known as *embodied energy*. For example, steel, used in virtually all modern construction, must be extracted from the earth in the form of iron ore, with machinery that in turn uses energy (fuel) to run. The raw material is then transported, perhaps hundreds of miles, for smelting, itself an energy-intensive process. The finished product—for instance, steel beams— is shipped a second time to a distribution center, and transported yet again to the build-

[21] World Resources Institute, op. cit. and World Resources Institute, *The 1993 Information Please Environmental Almanac* (Boston: Houghton Mifflin Company, 1993); *Environment on File* (New York: Facts on File, 1991).
[22] World Resources Institute, *World Resources 1992–1993*.

ing site, where it is hoisted into place. Each step requires the expenditure of more energy.

In theory it is possible to estimate the embodied energy in any material by knowing how much energy is used to extract and manufacture it, transport it to the building site. and install it. In practice, this is extremely difficult. It is possible, however, to apply a generalized set of comparisons to different types of materials and in so doing to make informed decisions about products and materials. For example:

1. Aluminum manufacture is a much more energy-intensive process than steel manufacture; therefore, all other factors being equal, aluminum would have more embodied energy and given a choice, steel would be the more energy-efficient choice.

2. All else being equal, a product transported over greater distances to reach a processing plant or building site would use more embodied energy and therefore be a less desirable choice than one transported a shorter distance.

3. Reusing or recycling material preserves embodied energy in two ways—first, because discarding the material results in the irretrievable loss of that energy, and second, because the energy required to create "virgin" material is almost always far greater than that required to recycle or reconstitute it. For example, it takes close to 7,000 Btu (British thermal units) to manufacture one aluminum can from scratch but less than half that energy—around 2,500 Btu—to recycle it.[23] Thus, all other things being equal, the use of recycled material whenever possible saves energy.

Besides consuming embodied energy, building also necessitates the direct consumption of natural resources. This in turn has a number of ramifications. First, few if any resources are inexhaustible, even so-called renewable resources. In the United States, for example, the voracious demand for wood products coupled with a dwin-

[23] World Resources Institute, *The 1993 Information Please Environmental Almanac.*

Life Cycle Summary: Steel

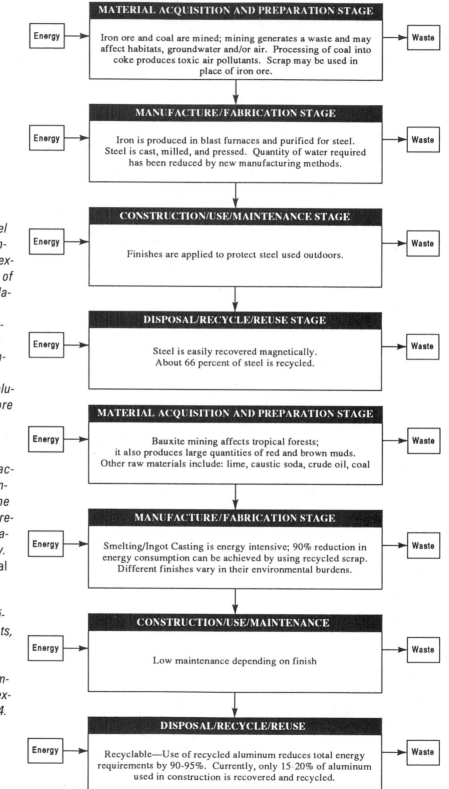

MATERIAL ACQUISITION AND PREPARATION STAGE

Iron ore and coal are mined; mining generates a waste and may affect habitats, groundwater and/or air. Processing of coal into coke produces toxic air pollutants. Scrap may be used in place of iron ore.

Energy → | → Waste

MANUFACTURE/FABRICATION STAGE

Iron is produced in blast furnaces and purified for steel. Steel is cast, milled, and pressed. Quantity of water required has been reduced by new manufacturing methods.

Energy → | → Waste

CONSTRUCTION/USE/MAINTENANCE STAGE

Finishes are applied to protect steel used outdoors.

Energy → | → Waste

DISPOSAL/RECYCLE/REUSE STAGE

Steel is easily recovered magnetically. About 66 percent of steel is recycled.

Energy → | → Waste

MATERIAL ACQUISITION AND PREPARATION STAGE

Bauxite mining affects tropical forests; it also produces large quantities of red and brown muds. Other raw materials include: lime, caustic soda, crude oil, coal

Energy → | → Waste

MANUFACTURE/FABRICATION STAGE

Smelting/Ingot Casting is energy intensive; 90% reduction in energy consumption can be achieved by using recycled scrap. Different finishes vary in their environmental burdens.

Energy → | → Waste

CONSTRUCTION/USE/MAINTENANCE

Low maintenance depending on finish

Energy → | → Waste

DISPOSAL/RECYCLE/REUSE

Recyclable—Use of recycled aluminum reduces total energy requirements by 90-95%. Currently, only 15-20% of aluminum used in construction is recovered and recycled.

Energy → | → Waste

Embodied energy in steel and aluminum. Energy inputs accumulate in the extraction and processing of any material; this cumulative energy is known as "embodied energy." Aluminum manufacture is a much more energy-intensive process than steel manufacture, and thus aluminum generally has more embodied energy than steel. However, factors such as transportation must also be taken into account. Waste is also generated at each step in the process. Recycling can recover all or most of a material's embodied energy. [From AIA, Environmental Resource Guide *(Apr. 1992).] Reproduced with permission of The American Institute of Architects, 1735 New York Avenue, NW, Washington, DC, 20006, under license number 93083. This license expires September 30, 1994. FURTHER REPRODUCTION IS PROHIBITED.*

dling resource base has exacerbated tensions in regions such as the Pacific Northwest whose economies have been built on the exploitation of these resources. The extraction of minerals, for example, has resulted in the degradation of millions of acres of landscape in this country alone and frequently pollutes the surrounding air and water. Despite stringent regulations, chemical manufacturers spew out countless airborne toxins and release contaminants into rivers and lakes. These chemicals will nonetheless find their way into buildings—in paints, dyes, adhesives, furniture, cleaning products, papers, and elsewhere.

The consumption of resources does not end with the construction of an office building. Indeed, the majority of consumption comes with the habitation and operation of an office building—the day-to-day functioning of office workers. This gives rise to yet another major environmental problem associated with office buildings—the disposal of solid waste. Office workers dispose of an esti-

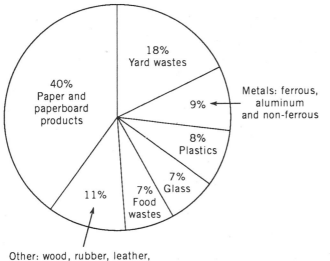

Breakdown of solid waste in the United States. Paper and paper products are the leading sources of solid waste. In office buildings they make up an even greater proportion of the waste stream. Recycling of paper will thus be crucial to any efforts at mitigating the growing "garbage crisis." (Data from Franklin Associates, Ltd.)

mated 250 pounds of garbage a year, 100 pounds of which is paper, the largest single component of solid waste. There are more than 10 million office workers in the United States generating a total of more than 1 billion pounds of wastepaper—the equivalent of 30 million trees.[24]

This unending stream of waste adds to the steadily increasing output of all solid waste in the United States. More than 210 million tons are disposed of annually, with roughly two-thirds going to landfills. At least half the landfills in the United States were estimated to have reached capacity by 1990.[25]

This state of affairs has resulted in many communities having to ship their garbage over long distances at great expense—or, as in the case of New York City, where the last open landfill is scheduled for closing within a few years, to plan construction of incinerators to handle the excess trash. Incinerators are fraught with political and environmental problems, however; their siting in predominantly low-income minority communities has stirred citizen outrage nationwide, and the emission and disposal of toxic pollutants from incinerators has not been adequately addressed. Recycling programs, which offer the best alternative to disposal and incineration, have received little impetus from either the federal or local governments. As a result, U.S. recycling rates are lower than those of most other industrialized countries.[26]

The Role of the Building Professional

It is clear from the foregoing discussion that every product employed in the construction, maintenance, or day-to-day functioning of an office building has environmental impacts that go far beyond its use. These impacts

---

[24] *Comparative Statistics of Industrial and Office Real Estate Markets.*
[25] World Resources Institute, *World Resources 1992–1993*; Cynthia Pollock, *Mining Urban Wastes: The Potential for Recycling* (Worldwatch Paper No. 76) (Washington, D.C.: Worldwatch Institute, 1987).
[26] Pollock, op. cit.

consist of "upstream" (before purchase) and "downstream" (after purchase) stages. Upstream impacts include extraction of raw materials, associated transportation, manufacturing processes, and distribution to the building site prior to construction or installation. Downstream impacts consist of operation, maintenance, and ultimately the method of disposal. The total flow of materials and energy through the built environment is shown schematically in the diagram in Appendix A, developed by Croxton Collaborative.

The biggest problem is that we architects have been using too narrow a balance sheet to evaluate our decisions. That sheet is not complete; it doesn't include total efficiency and environmental costs. A building may be cheap and pretty, but will it go on to become an environmental and financial burden to those who occupy and maintain it?

RANDOLPH CROXTON

Environmentalists are accustomed to thinking in terms of the entire life cycle of a product; that is, its existence and environmental impact from extraction through reuse or disposal. Architects and designers, on the other hand, have traditionally operated within the narrow period in a product's life cycle between its selection from the *Sweet's Catalog* and its incorporation into the working drawings. The well-meaning building professional rarely sees or deals with the upstream or downstream part of the equation of his or her choices—precisely where the greatest environmental impacts occur—thus unwittingly contributing to environmental degradation.

Unhealthy Offices

Perhaps the most insidious by-product of the built environment is *sick building syndrome* (SBS), a condition that occurs in as many as three of every ten office buildings in this country. SBS is indicated when occupants in a given building or location within a building report symptoms ranging from headache, dizziness, and nausea to respiratory distress and fatigue, but the exact nature or cause of the symptoms cannot be pinpointed. In general, SBS may arise from one or a combination of physical conditions common to many office buildings, particularly substandard indoor air quality, which can in turn be due to poor ventilation, a lack of adequate fresh air, or the buildup of noxious gases which are given off, or "off-gased," from furniture, glues, and other finishes. Bad lighting, workstations that are not designed ergonomically to promote good posture and comfort, an overly warm or cool indoor climate, and work-related stress can also contribute to SBS.[27]

A related condition, *building-related illness* (BRI), describes ailments that, unlike with SBS, can be traced directly to a specific air-quality problem within a building, such as poor ventilation.[28] The most notorious recent example of BRI is Legionnaire's disease, an infectious respiratory illness that was first identified in 1976 at a hotel in Philadelphia after 29 people had died. The bacterium that caused the outbreak was found to have accumulated in damp pockets of the building's ventilation ducts and been transmitted through the air-conditioning system.

Increasing attention has been focused on both SBS and BRI in recent years. Calculations have shown that SBS alone costs the U.S. economy roughly $60 billion a year in medical expenses and lost worker productivity. It is now widely accepted that the conventional standards of office construction of the last 20 years have mainly exacerbated rather than enhanced the quality of indoor office life. Office workers are increasingly trapped in sealed concrete and glass boxes with inadequate ventilation and infrequent air changes, surrounded by syn-

---

[27] U.S. Environmental Protection Agency (EPA) and National Institute for Occupational Safety and Health (NIOSH), *Building Air Quality: A Guide for Building Owners and Facility Managers* (Dec. 1991).
[28] Ibid.

thetic products that give off harmful gases. Little effort has been made to construct ventilation systems that go beyond minimum required specifications. Small wonder, then, that according to the U.S. Environmental Protection Agency, indoor air can be up to 100 times more polluted than outdoor air.

Philosophies of Wastefulness

If office buildings are in fact unhealthy energy- and resource-eating monsters, it makes sense to ask where expectations of building quality have gone wrong. At least a partial answer can be found in the priorities that dominated the "boom" in construction in the late 1970s and throughout the 1980s. Fast-growing businesses looked to developers to provide them with inexpensive, ready-to-occupy space, and developers in turn rewarded architects who could churn out inexpensive buildings in record time while complying with minimum building codes and standards. The "turnkey" or ready-made project became the dominant mode of building. Developers and their clients paid strict attention to the bottom line, even if it meant ignoring the physical discomforts of the building's occupants and the building's impact on the local or global environment.

The rise of modern building techniques and the accompanying modern aesthetic during the post–World War II years have abetted the move toward turnkey projects. Modernist design favored the sleek glass box and often paid little attention to site characteristics such as orientation or climate. The same design would be used for a project in Seattle, Singapore, or Stockholm, creating buildings that had much greater energy needs than those with site-specific design would have. Glass "curtain wall" construction may be easily exported but is seldom appropriate to the site.

Along with turnkey construction has come "overdesigning," by which a building's systems are designed to accommodate the greatest expected demand from present and future uses rather than being tailored to the specific needs of tenants. Thus it is not uncommon to find an office air-conditioning system with considerably more capacity than is actually demanded. As Audubon House dramatically demonstrates, such wasteful use of energy can be reduced easily.

The energy profligacy typical of building construction merely reflects the similar American attitude toward energy in general. Until fairly recently, the response to increasing demand for energy has been to provide the supply to meet it, if necessary by building more power plants. The United States has consistently lagged behind energy-efficient nations such as Germany and Japan, hurting its economy in the process. In the last few years, this trend has begun to change as utilities discover the competitive benefits of "demand-side" versus "supply-side" management. As energy efficiency and conservation proves to be less costly than construction, utilities are increasingly rewarding frugal consumers with rebates.

Another factor favoring the status quo has been the tendency among building professionals to regard energy efficiency and good indoor air quality with high levels of fresh air intake as two separate and irreconcilable goals. On one hand, where energy-saving heating, ventilation, and air-conditioning (HVAC) systems were used, indoor air quality actually suffered. On the other, advanced ventilation and filtration systems and greater fresh air ratios would require more energy and thus greater expense. This perceived dichotomy is illustrated by the fact that prior to 1990, the American Institute of Architects, the leading professional organization, had separate committees, frequently at odds, advocating indoor air quality versus energy concerns.

Whatever their causes, it is clear that the philosophies of wastefulness which have governed the bulk of building construction have created an unsatisfactory legacy: polluted cities, exhausted resources, a host of environmental threats such as ozone depletion and global warming, and unhappy and unhealthy workers. If we are to break out of this vicious cycle, new ways of thinking will have to supplant traditional "tried-and-true" techniques. Governments must set policies that provide incentives for the conservation of energy and resources and set high standards for public health and safety. Architects and designers must accept a greater degree of risk if they are to break through the barriers of the conventional without resorting to exotic expensive technology. Building owners and developers must understand that an overarching commitment to the environment is achievable with competitive, private, market-rate construction. These are the lessons embodied in Audubon House.

Dimensions of Sustainable Design

AUDUBON HOUSE REPRESENTS a major milestone in an ongoing progression. The endpoint of this progression—*sustainable* architecture and design—will occur when all buildings together minimize the use of energy and resources and the impacts of the built environment on natural systems and biodiversity, so as to guarantee their viability for future generations. To Audubon, sustainable architecture also rejects the notion that technology alone can correct environmental ills and find substitutes for resources that we squander. Sustainable architecture implies living within our means and finding practical solutions that can be implemented today. By itself, Audubon House cannot be considered "sustainable," but it does offer a model for turning to a future of building sustainably.

When work began on renovating the future Audubon House in early 1990, however, few precedents existed for such a project. The closest model, perhaps, was Croxton Collaborative's NRDC renovation, designed in 1988; however, that had been restricted to only three floors of an existing office building. William McDonough and a handful of architects were also developing elements of "green" commercial architecture, and there were a number of small-scale models, notably Amory Lovins's Rocky Mountain Institute, a kind of living laboratory of energy efficiency.

The Audubon project was more ambitious because it was to be carried out on a large-scale building renovation, allowing complete integration of the building's systems and design from the ground up. This gave the Audubon Team wide latitude to pursue its vision, defined by the architects as environmental, sustainable, and humanistic architecture. The pioneering nature of the Audubon project also meant that specific goals and guidelines to articulate them had to be developed along the way.

The renovation of Audubon House was less the systematic execution of a detailed, predetermined plan than it was an evolving process. Ideas as well as specific products and systems were tried and rejected as new and better information became available. Specific criteria for

---

The 'energy crisis' of the 1970s, coupled with the emergent environmental movement, produced two responses, or 'cultures,' in architecture. One, concerned mainly with reducing energy, utilized a high-technology approach to energy conservation; the other, concerned more with the widespread environmental impacts of development, used a low- or no-technology 'back to nature' approach. There was also a divide between energy conservation (which meant minimum fresh air) and improved indoor air quality (which required maximum fresh air and more energy). During the 1980s, common ground was established among these different points of view, illustrated in the 1988 redesign of the NRDC offices, where we were able to reconcile high levels of energy efficiency with high indoor air quality. In 1990, the American Institute of Architects, through the leadership of Bob Berkebile, merged the previously separate committees observing energy and indoor air quality, among others, to form the Committee on the Environment, which mirrors this 'holistic' perspective.

RANDOLPH CROXTON

the Audubon project were developed to meet the unique goals and needs of the society. Other criteria had to be followed as a result of Audubon's location and local and regional conditions and codes. Challenges came up that tested the resolve of team members to work cooperatively.

Nevertheless, the Audubon Team had an overarching set of objectives that guided the project from its inception, as well as a notion of how to meet these objectives. In this chapter we take a closer look at the goals of the Audubon project and the methodology used to carry them out.

Broadly speaking, the team's objectives were to design an office building that would be energy-efficient, environmentally sound, and both comfortable and healthy. The redesign would be accomplished at a competitive market rate, and the finished project would function as a "living model" for future projects. In addition, Audubon House had to take into account factors of safety, building and product performance, and aesthetics. It is in the careful balancing of all these considerations, while keeping the environmental (nontraditional) principles uppermost, that the key to the project can be found.

Environmental Goals

Foremost, Audubon House is designed to address those local and global environmental problems that are an outgrowth of the built environment, putting environmental criteria at the forefront of building decisions. Examples of global problems include climate change, ozone depletion, and loss of biodiversity. Local problems include both those environmental factors directly affecting office workers and their health, and issues particular to New York City or the Northeast region, such as the controversy over hydroelectricity development in the James Bay region of Canada.

The Audubon Team used general information about such issues to develop a loose set of environmental priorities for the project. The known impact of CFCs on ozone

Audubon House, sixth floor at start of renovation. By purchasing and renovating an entire office building, Audubon and its architectural team were able to incorporate environmental goals in an integrated fashion and in every aspect of the building process. (Photo by Otto Baitz.)

depletion and global warming, for instance, made the elimination of CFCs an obvious priority. Reducing demand for electricity was regarded as a high priority in order to give underpinning to Audubon's opposition to James Bay development. Whenever possible, the team also identified the specific direct environmental impacts as well as the indirect "upstream" and "downstream" impacts associated with each component of the building process. Overlaying this information on the set of environmental priorities—while also taking into account price, function, availability, and aesthetics—allowed the team to make informed design, purchase, and management decisions.

The environmental dimensions of Audubon House can be divided broadly into four major areas: energy conservation and efficiency; direct and indirect environmental impacts; high indoor air quality; and resource conservation and recycling. Although these areas overlap considerably, they provide a convenient framework for discussing the key environmental features of the project.

Energy Conservation and Efficiency. Because of the known impacts of energy consumption by the built environment, energy efficiency was an obvious priority. It was also one of the simplest areas in which significant reductions could be achieved.

Direct and Indirect Environmental Impacts. This category takes into account impacts associated not only with energy use, such as air pollution, but also those associated with the manufacture and use of building products, materials, and systems, such as water pollution and waste. Whenever possible, vendors were asked to provide detailed information on manufacturing processes, composition and content of materials, and factory location and conditions so that upstream and downstream impacts could be assessed and minimized.

Indoor Air Quality. The health and well-being of Audubon House and its occupants were of utmost importance, and the Audubon Team set out to create the healthiest and most comfortable offices possible (within the other constraints of the project). This goal has both environmental and humanistic dimensions; indoor air quality is the most clearly identifiable environmental consequence of a building's construction and operation, and good indoor air quality enhances employee satisfaction and productivity.

Resource Conservation and Recycling. Whenever feasible, the Audubon Team sought to minimize the use of natural resources in general, and of "virgin" natural resources in particular, by purchasing materials made with recycled content. Of equal, if not greater concern was the final disposition of materials—the question of solid waste. Audubon House addressed this concern with the installation and implementation of an advanced building recycling system.

In addition to these four major areas of·concern, two other factors deserve mention. In certain instances, the selection of natural materials was appropriate. For example, the carpeting chosen is 100 percent natural wool with no dyes; synthetic carpeting would have involved a more energy intensive manufacturing process and most likely dyes, which are highly polluting. However, natural products are by no means inherently superior to synthetic ones. In choosing furniture for meeting rooms, furthermore, the Audubon Team used the opportunity to encourage sustainable management of precious natural resources by selecting sustainably grown rainforest wood.

The Economic Imperative

If the "green" goals articulated at Audubon House are to be widely adopted by owners, developers, and building professionals, they need to satisfy other green goals—financial ones. This fact is critically important at present, when the public is demanding economic justifications for environmental programs. Audubon House was designed as a real-world model—to show that environmental design can indeed be achieved at a reasonable cost. The price tag for the renovation of Audubon House supports this assertion. The basic renovation and redesign cost $122 per square foot, well within the market rate (about $120 to $128 per square foot) for a project of comparable location, time, and size. Several anomalies of the project pushed the "fully loaded" cost to $142 (the largest one being a New York City law which stipulates that fire trucks must be able to drive onto the sidewalk; this required Audubon to replace the century-old vaulting beneath the sidewalk in front of the building), but

*Vaulting under sidewalk in front of Audubon House, Broadway side
of building. New York City law mandated extensive repairs to the underground vaulting, adding about 15 percent to the cost of the project. Even with this unexpected cost, the final price tag for renovation was just slightly above market rate—a key goal of the project.
(Photo by Otto Baitz.)*

this does not diminish the overall market-rate competitiveness of Audubon House.

For the project to end up at market rate, the Audubon Team developed a basic set of financial criteria to parallel the environmental ones. As a general principle, systems and products used at Audubon House had to be economically as well as environmentally justified. This entailed first looking at initial cost and *premium cost*—the price differential above a product or system with equivalent performance characteristics but lacking the environmental qualities. It also took into account durability and longevity of a system or product, its maintenance record, rebates (if any), cost of installation, and anticipated payback. In the course of the project, a number of more specific guidelines emerged that served as tests of cost-effectiveness. These were *not* hard and fast rules, however, but rather, "rules of thumb" to help gauge financial viability.

The most important guideline, applied to the energy-related systems, was the payback period—the amount of time it takes a system or systems to offset additional cost with accrued savings. *At Audubon House, payback was a standard of cumulative five-year maximum for all energy-related systems.* An extra "degree of difficulty" was added to the payback equation by comparing the premium cost of Audubon's efficient natural gas–fired heating, ventilation, and air conditioning (HVAC) system against a highly efficient electric-powered alternative (rather than the least costly code-compliant alternative).

Selection of an appropriate payback period was a critical step in making Audubon House a model. Typical turnkey projects have a payback period of one years or less, while corporate developments and institutions (schools, hospitals, government buildings, etc.) average two to three years. Audubon rejected these standards as shortsighted and because they would make it virtually impossible to achieve meaningful environmental performance. At the same time, however, Audubon did not want to set a standard that financially conscious owners and developers would perceive to be unreasonable or unattainable. Based on Croxton's experience at NRDC and a general sense of owners' expectations, the Audubon Team settled on the five-year payback—slightly more than the corporate and institutional standard and enough to allow a modicum of flexibility to achieve high environmental standards.

There are three broad overarching dimensions of value that drive the Audubon project: resource sustainability, environmental consequence, and the humanistic response. From these we derive the subsets related to recycling, energy efficiency, indoor air quality, pollution reduction, etc. No matter what the unique local characteristics of a project are—for instance the climate, utility fuel mix, geology, watershed—keeping these overarching concerns in mind will help the architect in any setting begin to organize priorities and come to the appropriate solutions for that site.

RANDOLPH CROXTON

The maximum five-year payback period established by the Audubon Team did have some notable consequences on subsequent building decisions. For example, the team modeled several scenarios for the rooftop installation of a solar photovoltaic (PV) array (composed of PV cells which convert sunlight directly into electricity). Despite the obvious environmental benefits of this renewable form of energy, its cost at the time was prohibitive; calculations performed by the team estimated that it would have taken more than 10 years to pay for itself, whereas substantial energy savings were indicated even without a PV system. As a result, the team decided not to install PV cells, but did leave an option for doing so once the technology becomes affordable.

From the start, to keep overall costs of the project down and promote the financial goals, the Audubon Team generally avoided the purchase of materials and products whose price was deemed unreasonably excessive, including those products chosen primarily for their contribution to indoor air quality or for recycled content. Later in the project, an attempt was made to put a quantitative value on this principle, which became known as the "10 percent test"—that is, items were avoided if their premium cost exceeded that of an average-priced alternative by greater than 10 percent. This test was applied loosely during the later stages of the project to "add-on" products, and it will also be used to evaluate future purchases of office supplies and equipment.

The team made some notable exceptions to this principle, however. If a product dramatically outperformed its "competitors" on environmental criteria, as was the case with the paint used in Audubon House, it was usually selected. Moreover, some materials (and strategies) were favored because they are likely to become more important and widely available in the near future. Such products were deployed symbolically, to underscore their potential of moving from "marginal" to "mainstream," and for demonstration purposes. Examples include the tiles used in the elevator vestibules (mainly of recycled glass); cable raceways at the base of workstation partitions (made without PVC plastics), and the food-waste composting program. Each of these involved considerable added expense but was deemed worthwhile to underscore the environmental goals of Audubon House.

Many of the environmental measures put in place at Audubon House have an added, hidden benefit: the avoidance of future costs. For example, simple devices installed to conserve water, such as low-flush toilets and faucets that shut off automatically, give Audubon a competitive edge in the event that water use in New York is metered—hardly an unlikely scenario, given the scarcity of the resource. (Many municipalities already charge for water use.) Audubon's ability to recycle most of its office waste precludes large "tipping" fees for waste disposal and could eventually turn a profit as the value of recyclable materials increases. And by situating its headquarters in a city with a well-established mass transit system, Audubon avoids having to pay for parking and other automobile-related expenses.

It is important to note that the financial criteria used by Audubon should not necessarily be followed verbatim by other owners. Aside from differences in an individual owner's financial situation, and hence ability to pay for desirable products, rapidly advancing manufacturing techniques and increased demand for green products is likely to make them increasingly affordable. Indeed, a key tenet of the Audubon project is that by encouraging the wider use of such products and materials, demand for them will increase, thus driving down costs.

Integrated Design and Practicability

To ensure that the techniques and principles used in its environmental renovation are practicable—that is, widely applicable to other projects and settings—the Audubon Team chose to purchase only "off-the-shelf" products and materials, those readily available to most practicing architects. No experimental or obscure items were used in Audubon House, although novel *uses* were found for traditional or previously little-used products. A rule of thumb was that a product had to have been on the market at least a year for Audubon to purchase it. This is not to say, however, that a fair degree of research may not be required to locate a product. Nonetheless, with a little extra legwork, practicing professionals should have no trouble locating desirable alternative products.

What makes Audubon House a particularly useful model is the fact that many of its solutions involve only the simplest of design methods. This holistic, or *integrated,* approach, developed by the architect and designer, named by the architects, is a hallmark of the Audubon project. Also known as "integrated, high-performance design," this system relies on the cumulative effects of no-cost or low-cost design solutions, in tandem with advanced technologies, to bring about the desired level of building performance. Perhaps its fullest expression is found in the integrated lighting scheme discussed in Chapter 4.

These two criteria, off-the-shelf technology and integrated design, work together. The integration of simple design techniques obviates the tendency toward piling on advanced, state-of-the-art gadgetry and ends up saving the owner thousands of dollars.

Balancing Factors and the "Ninety Percent Solution"

The factors that go into any building renovation or new construction are many and complex. Ideals of energy efficiency and environmental performance must constantly be weighed against not only cost considerations, but also aesthetic standards, humanistic goals (e.g., employees' comfort and pleasant ambience), and the day-to-day performance of the building and its components. Audubon House represents an attempt to balance all these factors while achieving a high overall level of environmental performance.

The design of Audubon House takes advantage of and enhances the building's greatest natural assets—access to sunlight and large floor-to-ceiling windows—to create an attractive, light-filled interior. The centerpiece of the design is the eighth-floor reception area, which is dominated by a large skylight and a wide staircase to the floor below. The area is also lit by windows that run the entire height from the seventh to eighth floors and that are framed by two-story columns, echoing the columns on the building facade. A highly styled, curved reception desk completes the effect by drawing the eye into the space.

Aside from its purely visual aspects, the design deliberately emphasizes the element of sunlight for its humanistic qualities. Light provides a feeling of connection with the outdoors and attunes us to the passage of time; it helps us locate our place in daily and seasonal cycles, instead of cutting us off from these natural rhythms. The design is also an extension of Croxton's earlier work at NRDC, where a dramatic, skylit staircase connecting three floors served as the communal focal point of the environmental redesign.

Main reception lobby, eighth floor. The skylight not only creates a light-filled space but also emphasizes the abundance of natural light and marks the natural rhythms of the day, themes that are central to the building project as a whole. (© Jeff Goldberg/ Esto.)

Another humanizing feature of Audubon House is the presence of operable windows. Actually, Audubon's energy-efficient and highly filtered HVAC system makes opening windows unnecessary (except in the unlikely event that the system fails) and even counterproductive—for example, it would permit unfiltered particulates to enter the building. But at the special request of Audubon President Berle, the option of opening windows was retained, allowing occupants the peace of mind that they have unrestricted access to the outside air and thus adding a human touch.

After much debate, perimeter offices were built along the western exposure of Audubon House. These, too, go

President's office with open windows. The choice of operable windows provides a "humanizing" touch to the workspace, allowing workers direct access to the outdoor environment and a degree of individualized "climate control" on temperate days. (© Jeff Goldberg/Esto.)

against purely energy-driven considerations because they potentially block daylight from the central floor spaces. Here again, though, the need of some staff for privacy outweighed other factors. The conflict was largely resolved by the installation of large windows in the offices' inner walls to allow the passage of light.

Construction of a ninth-floor conference center atop the existing building at 700 Broadway had a variety of architectural and humanistic incentives. The conference center is intended to be made available to small and medium-sized nonprofit groups as well as to Audubon staff. When fully completed, it will also open out onto a rooftop deck where employees and visitors will be able to sit and

enjoy the view. A rooftop garden will be added later, offering employees respite from the office routine; its plantings will be enhanced with compost from Audubon's composting project (see Chapter 7).

Inevitably, the balancing of many factors could not always be resolved in the most desirable way, and compromises had to be made at many points in the project. Properties of certain materials, structural characteristics of the building, or other contingencies sometimes made the choice of the best environmental alternatives difficult. For example, the poor condition of the floors in the corner of the building where the pantries are located necessitated using exterior-grade plywood subflooring

Ninth floor: conference center, skylight, and rooftop. Audubon commissioned construction of a ninth-floor conference center addition to the building. The conference center is available for use by other nonprofit organizations and adds value to the project for Audubon. Audubon employees have access to the rooftop, which is to be enhanced with plantings. (Photo by Otto Baitz.)

rather than the recycled material used elsewhere. Safety dictated that carpeting on stairways be glued in place; elsewhere, the carpeting was tacked, which helped to reduce the presence of toxins.

The Audubon Team implicitly recognized that such compromises were to be expected. Such an understanding is critical for any similar project to proceed and can be expressed as a "90 percent solution": It is inherently impossible to achieve total success, but achieving the highest possible success rate is more than sufficient to justify an environmentally driven project. In the final analysis, the environmental and human benefits of striving for an environmentally sound, energy-efficient design far outweighed any incidental shortcomings.

Teamwork: Redefining Roles

If integrated design was the essence of the architectural approach to Audubon House, teamwork was the essence of the human approach. Teamwork was indispensable to successful execution of the Audubon project, and it is the key to any similar undertaking. It necessitates the cooperation of all parties with a stake in the project, from the owner, architect, and designer on down to subcontractors. Each "player" must have a commitment to the overaching goals of the project. It is vitally important that building professionals develop a firm understanding of the environmental dimensions of their work, and it is equally important that environmentalists learn how to achieve their goals while remaining grounded in real-world considerations.

Real teamwork means thinking in new and different ways about the building process and the relationships of the building professionals involved. In conventional practice, a construction project proceeds from start to finish with limited interaction between architect and engineer, engineer and interior designer, lighting designer and architect, contractor and engineer, and so on. The architect and designer have primary responsibility for designing and coordinating the work, but some building systems are designed in isolation: choice and installation of the heating, cooling, and ventilation system, for example, are mainly at the discretion of the mechanical engineers; lighting designers select components of the lighting system; interior designers plan the layout and select decor and finishes. Each operates according to well-established criteria unique to his or her profession, with top priority usually given to lowest first cost or the creation of a particular "look." In this scenario, individual practitioners may, with the client's approval, set about achieving environmentally responsible design. Many engineers can and do seek to maximize indoor air quality and fresh air ratio, and interior designers may choose low-toxic furnishings. Yet these endeavors, undertaken in isolation, can be undermined by other decisions in the building as a whole.

The survival of the Earth's diverse ecosystems and the species that inhabit them, or 'biodiversity,' was the highest priority for Audubon. Ultimately, the steps taken at Audubon House to reduce environmental impacts and the consumption of energy and resources all come back to the issue of biodiversity.
JAN BEYEA

In contrast, Audubon House relied on a multidisciplinary approach, breaking down traditional barriers separating disciplines from one another and from the larger picture. This approach had been formalized previously at Croxton Collaborative, where leadership in architecture and interior design were vested in the firm's co-directors. At Audubon House, each member of the team had a clear idea of and commitment to the project's goals and parameters from the outset, as well as an understanding of how others' roles fit in. Thus, the architect and interior designer participated together in the initial planning, with the result that, for example, floor plans were arranged to take maximum advantage of natural light; similarly, the architect, engineers, lighting designer, and interior designer all cooperated to see that the selection of lamps and the placement of fixtures best suited the overall design scheme, that surfaces and finishes were arranged to get the most out of the lamps, and that the glazing (windows) had just the right level of transmissivity.

The role of the owner was of paramount importance in the Audubon project. Ultimately, it was up to Audubon's leadership to set the overarching goals of the project, establish the financial terms, hire the building professionals, and resolve disputes. The project benefited immeasurably from the greater-than-normal input of the owner as well as from Audubon's environmental expertise.

A commitment to teamwork is not without its challenges, as Audubon discovered. Sometimes serious disagreements arose. Some of these are common to building projects everywhere, such as tension between the owner's representative, who monitored the project budget, and the architect over design solutions and risks in the nontraditional uses of materials. When a spirit of cooperation prevailed, however, these conflicts often led to new solutions that satisfied both the architect's and owner's concerns. This spirit of cooperation extended to all levels of the project. In fact, a reception was held at the contractor's offices at which the architect and other team members reiterated the goals of the project and pointed out to the subcontractors the competitive advantage to be gained by acquiring skills with new materials and striving for environmental performance. With the subcontractors fully committed to the project, many potential tensions were avoided.

The Environmental Expert

When we think about the construction of a building, we usually think of architects, designers, and engineers. But the pursuit of environmentally sound building practices has brought to the fore a new kind of building professional, the environmental expert. The Audubon Team was lucky to have an architect and designer who had expertise of their own in environmental and sustainable concepts and who had gained considerable experience in earlier projects in researching and evaluating environmental products and systems. Even so, the presence of an Audubon staff expert, the society's chief scientist, was crucial to the project.

In searching for professionals to work on Audubon House, we used several guidelines. Each team member was expected to have a broad understanding of and commitment to environmental and energy issues; a basic grasp of manufacturing processes; the ability and commitment to conduct research; and above all a willingness to work in an integrated fashion with other team members. In particular, we looked for an architect who could conceptualize beyond the material design—a viewpoint not trapped by the purely aesthetic.

PETER A. A. BERLE

For example, the Audubon expert played a pivotal role in the analysis and selection of materials, having had extensive training in analyzing chemical components and their human-health effects. Many of these choices required very fine judgments and painstaking analyses of the relative environmental impacts of different materials. As an environmentalist, the Audubon expert was accustomed to looking at the upstream and downstream impacts associated with different products, was familiar with a wide range of environmental issues, and had special expertise in energy issues. Finally, since the completion of Audubon House, the Audubon expert has had the major responsibility for carrying forward the environmental goals of the project to the daily operation and maintenance of the building.

As building practices evolve to be more environmentally aware, architects and designers will increasingly need the services of an environmental expert. The environmental consultant will be in a position to offer advice on key decisions, such as how to balance economic factors with potential environmental gains and how to compare trade-offs when different environmental issues are at stake: indoor air quality issues, local environmental priorities, interpretation of chemical data, and trends in environmental protection. Most important, the expert will help establish credibility that professional environmental judgments have been made.

Although the Audubon Team had at its disposal in-house environmental expertise, most building professionals will need to locate professional environmental consultants from private practice, other environmental groups, or university environmental studies programs. The AIA Committee on the Environment may also be able to recommend experts, particularly in the area of indoor air quality.

The combination of enlightened owner, architect, designer, engineer, and environmental consultant was the key to Audubon's success. Using this team approach can unlock the potential for any building to match or exceed Audubon's standards.

The Role of Computer Modeling

Traditional engineering calculations, which measure such elements as a building's volume, heating and cooling capacity, and lighting load, can be used to make general estimates of a project's energy needs, but their ability to produce a detailed energy profile is severely limited. Modern energy-efficient design depends increasingly on sophisticated computer technology to fill in the gaps. Computer software programs developed or refined in recent years can provide highly accurate estimates of energy needs and usage by simulating real-life conditions that incorporate many more variables than traditional models. One such program, DOE-2, developed by the U.S. Department of Energy and the Electric Power Research Institute of California, was employed by the Audubon Team to substantiate the initial estimates of the building's energy usage and to help integrate add-ons into the building's design and systems.

Previously, DOE-2 had been employed almost exclusively in the public sector to establish compliance with existing building and energy codes. The Audubon Team used it largely to demonstrate how cost-effective, energy-saving design could perform far beyond code. Run in combination with readily available software extensions, DOE-2 helped the team calculate the interplay of fundamental building components, such as the thermal shell and insulation, the HVAC and electrical systems, and lighting load, with a wide assortment of other energy-

Eighth-floor interior, looking west along the southern exposure. Abundant natural light floods the interior from the southern and western exposures, dramatically reducing the need for electrical lighting. Use of DOE-2 computer software helped confirm the energy savings to be gained from "daylighting" the interior. (Photo by Otto Baitz.)

Interior, typical window with venetian blinds. These unique blinds have tiny pinholes in the slats that allow diffuse light to penetrate. When the product came on the market midway through the project, the DOE-2 software indicated that the energy savings resulting from its installation would justify the premium cost. (Photo by Otto Baitz.)

related factors and devices, including the building site, weather patterns, incoming daylight and shadows, glazing, lighting ballasts, and reflectance of interior surfaces. Further, by factoring in local utility rates, DOE-2 was able to compute the relative financial savings associated with overall energy efficiency and individual energy-saving devices. (See Appendix B.)

The use of DOE-2 facilitated several design changes and decisions during the course of the renovation. For example, a DOE-2 analysis established the superiority of one model of heat-mirror™ window over another. It also confirmed the benefits of adding a night cooling (passive solar) strategy to the building's heating and cooling system. Using DOE-2, Audubon ultimately projected that the cumulative energy-saving strategies would result in a building 64 percent more efficient than a conventional, code-compliant approach to the building would have produced.

The cost of the full DOE-2 analysis was prohibitive at the time of the Audubon project, but the architect proposed a study-grant, which led Con Edison, the conservation-minded local utility, to donate funds for the program, convincing them that DOE-2 could firmly establish the massive conservation potentials in the building renovation market. Less expensive software packages that make similar building-efficiency calculations are now coming on the market or under development, such as the Advanced Energy Design and Operation Technologies (AEDOT) system developed for the Department of Energy by the Pacific Northwest Laboratory. The American Institute of Architects and other groups are actively working to make this type of computer program widely available to building professionals.

The dimensions of sustainable design are many and multifaceted. They include conceptual dimensions based on a clear set of environmentally driven goals and values and human dimensions of cooperation and teamwork. There is no blueprint for sustainable design, and the professional judgments and values of the participants in any such project must be brought to bear on the decision-making process.

Audubon House is not a "perfect" building; indeed, no building can be perfect. But the combination of design strategies and technologies used at Audubon House achieve high standards of energy efficiency and environmental performance, at market rates. In the next section we examine in more detail the systems and strategies that make Audubon House work.

PART

II

INSIDE AUDUBON HOUSE

Systems and Strategies

Audubon House, schematic diagram showing integrated environmental approach. The integrated approach is based on coordinated planning of architectural, interior design, lighting, and mechanical engineering components of the building to produce the desired environmental and energy-efficient results. (Courtesy of Croxton Collaborative, Architects.)

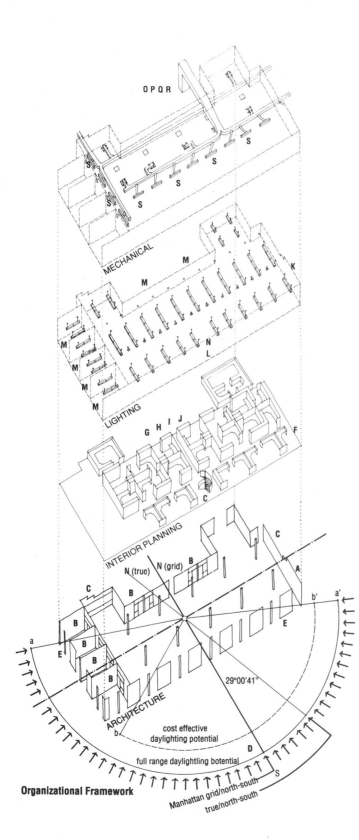

Organizational Framework

Mechanical Components

O High efficiency gas-fired absorption heater/chiller serves air handler at each floor.

P Separate, mandated outside air system delivers 24 cfm per person.

Q Number of air changes (recirculated and filtered air) is 6.2 per hour.

R Moisture carry-through in system is minimized by low velocity (less than 500 fpm) as well as cooling coil configuration.

S Variable volume units at each perimeter office assure individual control and their arrangement in open office assures full "mixing" of air.

Lighting Components

K Daylighting photocell controls outer bay of lighting (full range dimming)

L All lighting is high efficiency, high color rendition fluorescent with electronic ballast (one ballast for two fixtures).

M Sensors at offices, conference room, etc., turn off lights when room is unoccupied (zone sensors for open area).

N Pendant arrangement of single tube fixtures with up/down components achieves 30 fc ambient light level with low glare characteristics overall.

Interior Planning Components

F Perimeter work stations are held to 3 ft. 6 in. to maximize daylight to interior.

G Open office area is organized east/west to take maximum advantage of daylighting.

H Colors for systems furniture and interior surfaces are in high reflectance range to maximize both natural and artificial light.

I Task lighting is incorporated as part of high efficiency task/ambient system.

J All work stations meet test method and criteria for offgassing of formaldehyde, volatile organic compounds, particulates, etc.

Architectural Components

A Full-height ceiling maintained at building perimeter to maximize daylight effect.

B Enclosed office grouped north and west with clerestory glass.

C Core elements (elevators, fire stairs, pantry and mechanical rooms) on north and east solid exterior walls.

D High thermal performance windows with high transmissivity of natural light.

E Exterior wall thermal upgrade (insulation) approximately three times code requirement (applies to all exterior walls)

Lighting and Other Energy Efficiencies

4

AUDUBON HOUSE ACHIEVES dramatic reductions in energy consumption principally from two areas: decreased need for artificial lighting and an upgraded thermal shell. These reductions are accomplished within the specified payback period of five years and with an increase, not decrease, in employee comfort. Nor are aesthetic standards compromised—Audubon House's light-filled interiors embody a memorable visual quality.

In the average American office, 30 to 40 cents out of every dollar spent on energy goes to lighting. Paying for lighting energy is thus clearly among the top expenses of doing business. Nationwide, lighting for buildings, both commercial and residential, is the largest source of electrical demand and thus a major environmental liability. It is likely that more than half of that lighting energy is wasted simply as a result of overlit offices, inefficient lamps and ballasts, badly designed fixtures, and lights that remain on unnecessarily. The good news is that lighting is the most easily mitigated cost. In fact, by using natural light more effectively, distributing light more sensibly, and integrating readily available, high-performance lighting components, Audubon slashed its need for lighting electricity by more than *75 percent.* Bringing in abundant natural light also provided employees a psy-

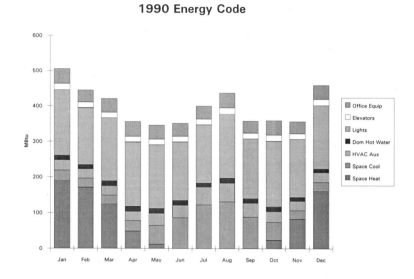

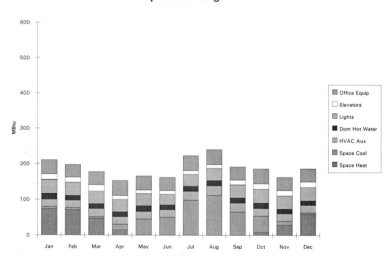

Monthly energy use by building components. Based on output by the DOE-2 software. These figures allowed the Audubon Team to assess where the greatest potential existed for energy efficiency. (Courtesy of Energy Simulation Specialists.)

chological lift and helped orient them to the passage of time and seasons.

Upgrading the thermal shell of a building to maximize insulation has been aided by a steady advance in building codes and even more by rapid advances in window and insulation technology. Much of this technology is available to homeowners and commercial builders alike. Although retrofitting the insulation in an already occupied building may be difficult, replacing windows alone can make a big difference. Owners and architects undertaking new construction or renovation have a wide variety of options for insulation available to them.

Designing with Light

More than any other feature of Audubon House, the lighting design clearly illustrates the simplicity and advantages of an integrated approach, by which inexpensive design decisions create significant cumulative savings of energy and money. Audubon House is blessed with an abundance of natural light to begin with: large floor-to-ceiling windows dominate the south and west exposures of the building, the two best directions for sunlight. (Because other buildings are directly adjacent to Audubon House, there are no windows on its north or east sides.) The Audubon Team took full advantage of the natural light by devising an open floor plan that matches the south and west orientation of the building exterior, thus "daylighting" the building—allowing the maximum penetration of daylight throughout the space. This was to be in essence an "office without walls."

The open plan was largely adhered to in the final execution of the design, but it was altered in the course of the project with the addition of perimeter offices along the western exposure to accommodate staff who needed higher levels of privacy and quiet. To compensate, the inward-facing walls of these offices were each fitted with two large windows—a clerestory over the door and a window adjacent to the door—so that sunlight could still penetrate the large central open space on each floor. The

Installation of windows. Floor-to-ceiling windows on the southern and western exposures of Audubon House ensured an abundance of natural light. The windows themselves use heat-mirror™ technology to achieve a high level of insulation. (Photo by Otto Baitz.)

open plan features a grid of spacious employee work-stations divided by sound-absorbing partitions. Partitions located closest and perpendicular to the windows are approximately 4 feet high (51 inches), while those farther away from the windows are a little over 5 feet high (63 inches). This subtle design feature, along with the stepping of the ceiling in the overhead plane, prevents the outer partitions from blocking more sunlight, further brightening the entire space.

To enhance the daylighting of the interior, only white to midrange finishes are selected for all surfaces, maximizing the reflectance of natural light. Walls and ceilings are painted or shop-finished in soft white. The parti-

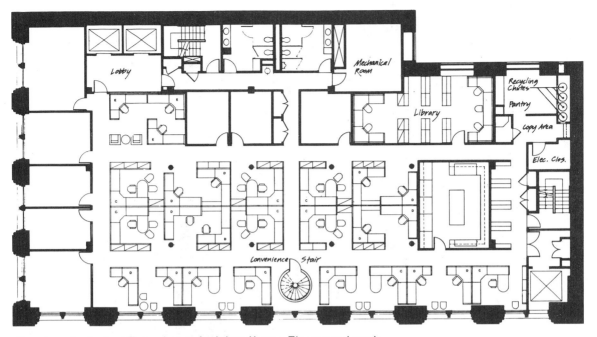

Drawing of a typical floor plan at Audubon House. The central workspaces feature open plans with modular workstations, enhancing the daylighting of the interior. Enclosed offices are grouped along the western and northern perimeters, minimizing interference with daylighting, and core elements (elevators, fire stairs, pantries, and mechanical rooms) are grouped on the north and east solid exterior walls, away from the sunlit southern and western exposures. (Courtesy of Croxton Collaborative, Architects.)

tions and carpeting average midrange taupe, as do file cabinets and workstation cabinets; workstation desktops are off-white; and most chairs are in bright colors with floral patterns. Wall decorations (from Audubon's own collection) are hung in key locations throughout the building to keep as much as possible of the white wall surface uncovered.

One of the most striking features of the lighting design at Audubon House is the way in which the light is distributed. Many office buildings typically deploy uniform "ambient," or background, light throughout the interior, at a level of brightness between 50 and 70 footcandles. (Brightness of lighting is measured in lumens and foot-

Interior, typical central workspace. Notice that the workspace partitions along the perimeters are shorter than those away from window, allowing daylight to penetrate. Walls, floors, and furnishings are all finished in light colors for greatest reflectance of natural light. (Courtesy of Bernstein Associates.)

candles. A *lumen* is the light emitted by a uniform point source, such as a light bulb, and is about equivalent to the light of one candle; a *footcandle* is a unit of illuminance on a surface, and is the result of one lumen uniformly striking a surface one square foot in area.) Ironically, this glaringly bright, even level of ambient light, because it bears no relationship to the layout of workspaces, is often insufficient for task work, so workers supplement it with individual incandescent desk lamps. It is also a potent source of eyestrain, discomfort, and fatigue. (Audubon staff who worked in the previous

Overview of a central workspace area, showing modular workstations. The architectural elements and interior design of the renovation were carefully coordinated to take maximum advantage of daylight, orienting the positions of offices and workstations for full daylighting potential. (Photo by Tom Mead.)

headquarters knew this well, and it was not uncommon to find an employee who had disconnected the overhead fluorescent lights and purchased his or her own desk lamp instead.)

The designers of Audubon House used a "task/ambient" approach that eschews the uniform production of ambient light and instead delivers light to where it is needed. The overall ambient light level is reduced to just 25 to 30 footcandles and supplemented by systems task lights built into the modular workstations. These desk lights use fluorescent lamps identical to the overhead

Interior workstation showing task/ambient lighting system. Unlike conventional offices, Audubon House employs a greatly reduced level of ambient (background) light, while built-in task lights in each workstation provide directed light for working. Both the task and ambient lights use high-efficiency tri-phosphor fluorescent lamps that produce natural colors. The task lights feature a three-way switch to adjust brightness. (Photo by Otto Baitz.)

lamps and are fitted with a three-way switch that gives the user an option of up to 70 footcandles. In addition, area lighting in the eighth-floor reception area, elevator vestibules, and stairways uses individual compact fluorescent lights.

Instead of being recessed into ceiling fixtures, the overhead lights at Audubon House consist of pendant (hanging) fixtures made with aluminum, fitted with 4-foot-long fluorescent lamps (see the accompanying dia-

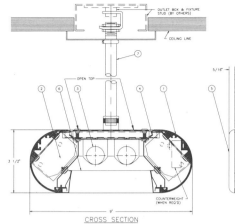

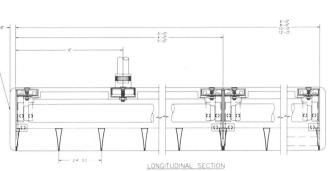

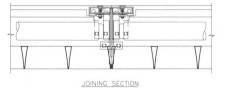

LINEAR LIGHTING CORP.

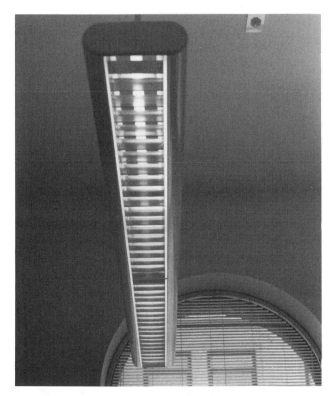

Typical ambient light fixture and lamp, technical drawing. The pendant (hanging) fixture, open on top and bottom, provides nearly 360° dispersal of the light. The high-efficiency T-8 lamp is fired by an electronic blast that further boosts efficiency and virtually eliminates flicker. (Drawing courtesy of Linear Lighting Corp.)

Photo by Tom Mead.

gram). The fixtures come in 4-, 8-, and 12-foot lengths and have one, two, or three single lamps, respectively. These fixtures hang approximately 2 feet from the ceiling and are open on top and bottom to allow nearly a 360-degree dispersal of the light. Parabolic reflectors built into the fixtures and a high-reflectance (88 percent) aluminum coating aid in the dispersal of the light. Because of the task/ambient lighting strategy and enhanced dispersal of the fixtures, the overhead lights at Audubon House are spaced on average 8 to 10 feet apart in open areas, a remarkable reduction in overall lighting needs compared to typical offices.

Lighting Technologies and Controls

The Audubon Team selected high-efficiency (T-8) fluorescent lamps for the task and ambient lighting in place of the conventional (T-12) fluorescents found in most commercial buildings. (The "T" stands for tubular; the numeral is the diameter of the tube in eighths of an inch; hence a "T-8" lamp is a tube 1 inch in diameter, and "T-12" is $1\frac{1}{2}$ inches in diameter.) The advanced T-8 lamps are designed to use 32 watts, compared to 40 watts in T-12 lamps. Moreover, they produce approximately 10 percent more lumens (brightness) per watt, in part because of their smaller diameter.

Not only are the lights used at Audubon House more energy efficient than conventional ones, but they produce a more pleasant illumination. Standard fluorescents produce a cold white light. The inside of the T-8 lamps at Audubon House are treated with a "triphosphor" coating, which permits a larger portion of the visible spectrum to be utilized, creating a more natural light (31 kelvin at Audubon House), closer in tone to daylight than that of conventional fluorescents.

Audubon's ambient lights are fired by electronic ballasts rather than standard magnetic, or core-coil, ballasts. (Ballasts are devices that provide the startup current to the tube.) The newer electronic ballasts increase the efficiency of the lights and can fire more than one lamp apiece, reducing the energy usage in a typical two-lamp fixture from 64 watts to 60 watts (a 6 percent gain in efficiency). They also fire at a much higher frequency than magnetic ballasts—more than 20,000 cycles a second as compared to the 60 cycles a second in standard models. This adds to higher-quality light by eliminating the distracting "flicker" and "hum" of conventional fluorescents.

Lighting is the simplest area in which to make substantial energy-saving decisions. If architects or designers were to do only one thing to make a building more energy efficient, I would suggest they look at the lighting design.
KIRSTEN CHILDS, DIRECTOR OF INTERIOR DESIGN,
CROXTON COLLABORATIVE

The combination of high-efficiency lamps and state-of-the-art electronic ballasts makes each ambient light fixture at Audubon House extremely energy efficient. Whereas a conventional fluorescent fixture of equivalent size would use 84 watts, those at Audubon House use just 60 watts—an energy savings of 30 percent.

The task lighting built into the workstation modules also utilizes T-8 triphosphor lamps, ranging from $1\frac{1}{2}$ to 4 feet long. These lamps were preinstalled by the furniture manufacturer. The designers believed it was important to match the color of the task lights to those of the ambient lights, and when the initial lamps arrived with the incorrect though standard K41 color rating, they were returned to the manufacturer, who replaced them with lamps bearing the correct specifications.

As noted previously, lighting in several areas (and desk lamps, where needed) is provided by compact fluorescent bulbs, which were inexpensive to purchase because of generous rebates by Con Edison. These bulbs perform both a practical and a symbolic function. Each bulb uses on average 75 percent less energy, in part because it is

10 times more long-lived, than a standard incandescent light bulb.[29] Since compact fluorescents are widely available as a consumer item, their use at Audubon House will hopefully encourage greater use in residential and commercial buildings. Audubon House uses no incandescent bulbs whatsoever.

The savings to Audubon from the lighting design alone will pay back the initial investment in less than three years, and this savings will continue to grow dramatically as energy costs climb.
RANDOLPH CROXTON

Along with the basic lighting components, two lighting "controls" are used at Audubon House that add phenomenally to the building's overall energy savings. Occupancy sensors, or motion detectors, ensure that lights are not left on unnecessarily. If a sensor does not detect motion in a given area for 6 minutes, the overhead lights switch off automatically. Occupancy sensors were installed in all open areas and all but a few offices and conference rooms. It is estimated that the use of this technology alone will reduce total electricity demand at Audubon House by 30 percent.[30]

Daylight dimming sensors were installed for the first row of lights in the open spaces along the building's southern exposure. Photocells in these small sensors read the amount of incoming daylight reflecting off work surfaces and signal the electronic ballasts to adjust the level of artificial light accordingly to maintain an even 25 to 30 footcandles of ambient light. Thus, the brighter the daylight, the lower the level of artificial ambient light and the greater the savings. These devices were an "add-alternate" item in the initial plans—that is, they were not considered an essential item but were on the "wish list"

---

[29] Barbara Burge, "Super-bulbs Brighten Outlook for Energy Savings at Home," *Audubon Activist* (Dec. 1990).
[30] Based on first-year figures from the Natural Resources Defense Council.

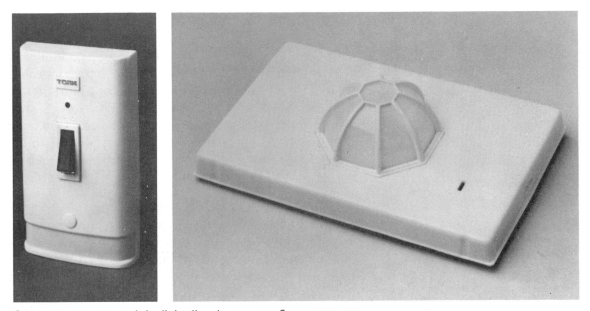

Occupancy sensor and daylight dimming sensor. Occupancy sensors (strip at bottom), which automatically switch off lights if no motion is detected after 6 minutes, are installed in almost all offices and workspaces at Audubon House. Daylight dimming sensors are installed along the southern exposure. These devices adjust the level of ambient lighting in response to the level of incoming daylight. Use of these two control devices alone saves more than 0.4 watt per square foot, almost half of what the wattage would be without them. (Courtesy of Tork.)

of features. But a simulation with the DOE-2 software indicated that the large amount of daylight entering from the south presented an opportunity for further savings, more than making up for the expense of the sensors. Because less daylight entered on the west side of the building, savings there would have been minimal, so the team did not install the devices there.

Venetian blinds at Audubon House were another add-alternate feature. Tiny perforations in the slats allow these blinds to block out bright light while permitting a soft daylight to penetrate. This gives occupants control of glare from direct sunlight without eliminating all of the daylighting contribution.

Insulation and Windows

Any attempt to improve a building's energy efficiency must begin with the thermal shell: the exterior walls, roof (and skylights), and glazing (windows). Audubon House was no exception. The building's exterior was structurally sound, but like most older buildings, its only insulation was the masonry walls themselves. The Audubon Team immediately set out to retrofit the building with high-performance insulation.

The typical lighting fixture you find in most office buildings consists of an array of fluorescent tubes recessed into the ceiling and covered by a plastic lens. As a consequence, a lot of light is absorbed inside the fixture and never reaches the space where it belongs. That's an incredible waste of energy. Our design negates that problem with open pendant fixtures, reducing glare and concentrations of light while maintaining a level of ambient light with a more residential feeling.

RANDOLPH CROXTON

In the search for effective commercial insulation, however, crucial environmental factors came into play. The two most common types of insulation on the market are foam insulation and rigid fiberglass. Foam insulation is a form of plastic usually manufactured with and containing chlorofluorcarbons (CFCs) or hydrochlorofluorocarbons (HCFCs). When emitted into the atmosphere, these compounds become the leading cause of stratospheric ozone depletion, and they are believed to cause up to 25 percent of the greenhouse effect, or global warming. Other foam insulations offgas formaldehyde and contain harmful chemicals. Fiberglass, however, contains small particles that can cause respiratory irritation if released into the air.

Neither foam nor fiberglass seemed satisfactory, but the Audubon Team seemed to be confronted with Hobson's choice—until the designer discovered a new product on the market called Air-Krete™. This insulation is a cementatious (cementlike) foam made of magnesium compounds (extracted from seawater) mixed with dolomite and other minerals. It was air-blown as a wet foam into the newly created cavity walls at Audubon House, where its use is thought to be among the first commercial-scale applications of this insulation—and proves the enormous value of patience and persistence! (Because it is blown in as a wet foam, this insulation could not be installed horizontally, so on the roof rigid fiberglass insulation was substituted.)

Air-Krete® insulation in cavity wall. This high-efficiency cementatious foam insulation is blown into the wall, where it hardens. It is made with magnesium compounds extracted from seawater and contains no chlorofluorocarbons (CFCs), which contribute to ozone loss and global warming. (Photo by Otto Baitz.)

Finding energy-efficient windows proved a simpler task. Window technology has advanced rapidly in the past decade or so, and prices of the most advanced windows are competitive. Audubon's windows use Heat-Mirror™ technology: Suspended between two panes of glass is a low-emissivity (low-e) and wavelength-selective coated film (shade coefficient = 0.41, with a daylight transmittance of 53 percent) that deflects the majority of sun's radiant heat outward, keeping the interior cool in summer, and deflects convector radiant heat inward, conserving heat in winter. The skylight glazing of tempered glass also uses heat-mirror™ technology but has a lower daylight transmittance (45 percent) associated with its ability to reduce higher levels of heat gain.

The perforated venetian blinds installed at Audubon House are a perfect example of an aesthetically pleasing and ingenious energy-saving technology; simply by having tiny perforations in the slats, these blinds create the option to block out the sun's direct beam light, while letting in a diffuse light, rather than reflecting all the sunlight back outside. When the blinds are closed, it is possible to still see the outline of the cityscape outside.

KIRSTEN CHILDS

The windows at Audubon have an insulation value, or *R,* of 3.7 (*U* = .27), equivalent to that of a standard brick wall. (*R* is the measure of a material's resistance to conducting heat; the higher the number, the greater the resistance, or insulation.[31]) Newer models on the market achieve values of *R*-8 or higher. The windows are highly insulated, with a rubberized thermal break which helps minimize the transfer of cold (or heat) from the exterior to the interior, and vice-versa.

[31]*R* value is expressed as °F ft^2/Btu per hour. *U* value is expressed as Btu per hour/ft^2 per °F. A Btu, or British thermal unit, is a measure of the quantity of heat required to raise the temperature of one pound of water one degree Fahrenheit at 39.2°F, or the approximate equivalent of one burning wooden match tip.

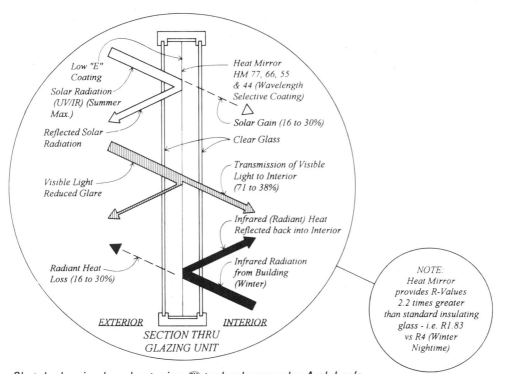

Sketch showing how heat mirror™ technology works. Audubon's high-efficiency windows feature this technology—a polymer film suspended between two panes of glass. The chemically treated film is wavelength-selective, resisting the transfer of heat through the windows. (Courtesy of Croxton Collaborative, Architects.)

Overall, the walls at Audubon House achieve an *R*-value of greater than 12, far beyond the New York state code (*R* = 3) allowable at the time of construction. The roof is also much more highly insulated than required by code (*R* > 33), as compared to code (*R* = 12). Thus Audubon House is thermally sound, and very little energy gets wasted.

Environmental and Economic Benefits

The magnitude of the energy savings represented by the use of daylighting, efficient lighting systems, and insulation cannot be overstated, nor can the environmental and financial benefits. The "connected lighting load" at Audubon House—that is, the maximum energy use *without* the added controls—is 0.97 watt per square foot, less than half of what a New York City code-compliant building would use (2.4). With the controls (the occupancy sensors and daylight dimmers) factored in, that figure falls by as much as half, to between *0.6 and 0.7 watts per square foot,* or as much as 80 percent less than the energy use of a code-compliant building. In large part

Installation of high-efficiency windows. The windows at Audubon House have an insulation value close to R-4, equivalent to that of a brick wall. Newer models achieve R-8 or greater. The overall insulation of Audubon's thermal shell exceeded the code at the time of construction by as much as 80 percent. (Photo by Otto Baitz.)

because of the lighting reductions, Audubon's overall peak electricity demand—the amount of electricity consumed during periods of greatest use—is 68 percent less than that of a code-compliant building.

The additional first cost, or premium cost, of the lighting system was approximately $92,000, about a quarter of which was for the energy-efficient ballasts and controls. The direct electricity savings from the system are projected at about $60,000 a year. By installing energy-efficient lighting equipment, moreover, Audubon received $31,000 in rebates from Con Edison, the local utility. The approximate payback for the lighting system at Audubon House is two and a half years.

(Besides helping Audubon offset first costs, these equipment-based rebates benefit the utility. The savings from "demand management" far outweigh the costs of supplying more and more energy. In the future, it is anticipated that rebates will be offered based on performance (i.e., the cumulative reduction in electricity usage rather than equipment. Had this been the case at the time of the Audubon project, Audubon would have qualified for even greater rebates.)

A well-insulated thermal shell is key to an energy-efficient building. Otherwise, all your energy savings will just go right out the window.
JORDAN FOX, FLACK + KURTZ CONSULTING ENGINEERS

Some sense of the environmental benefits of the reduced energy consumption at Audubon House can be gleaned from the following statistic: Replacing just a single conventional light switch with an occupancy sensor saves 950 kilowatthours—preventing pollution equivalent to 1,500 pounds of carbon dioxide, 11 pounds of sulfur dioxide, and 6 pounds of nitrogen oxides a year.[32] Calculations prepared by the Natural Resources Defense Council, based on energy reductions like those at Audubon House, provide an even more dramatic picture of

---

[32] U.S. Environmental Protection Agency, *Green Lights Program.*

the environmental gains. NRDC estimated that if energy savings of similar magnitude were adopted by the commercial sector nationwide over the next 20 years, the United States would save 40,000 megawatts of baseload capacity, avoid emitting 175 million tons of carbon dioxide a year into the atmosphere (more than 3 percent of current U.S. carbon dioxide emissions), eliminate the need for 85 percent of currently operating nuclear plants, and save the economy $60 to $80 billion.[33]

Not to be overlooked are the direct benefits of the high-quality naturalistic light at Audubon House, which is anticipated to reduce eyestrain, headache, fatigue, and related symptoms while increasing worker productivity. The decreased demand for lighting also significantly reduced the contribution of the lighting to the building's heating load, helping to reduce the demand for cooling the building.

The upgrade of the thermal shell played a complementary role in the drastic downsizing of the heating and cooling equipment installed in Audubon House. Simulations performed on the DOE-2 software confirmed that without the thermal upgrade and increased lighting efficiency, the building would have needed a 350-ton-capacity unit; with the upgrade (and other energy improvements), a unit with a 180-ton capacity was sufficient—with room to spare.[34] At least 40 percent was saved by the lighting design, the balance by the thermal shell, windows, and other strategies. The heating and cooling needs of Audubon House were thus effectively cut in half by good insulation and design measures.

Largely as a result of both of these features—the equipment downsizing and the lighting reductions—Audubon House is estimated to use 62 percent less overall energy than would be used by a code-compliant building and save 64 percent in energy costs, or about $100,000 a year. The final component in this equation is the HVAC system itself—the subject of the next chapter.

---

[33] Natural Resources Defense Council, pers. comm.
[34] A ton of heating capacity is equal to 12,000 Btu.

Heating, Cooling, and Energy at Audubon

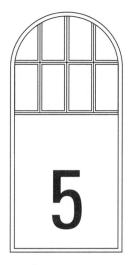

5

MOST OFFICES, COMMERCIAL BUILDINGS, and homes in the United States that require both heating and cooling have separate systems. Typical heating systems are powered by burning fuel oil or natural gas on-site or from electricity generated off-site. In New York City, much heating in commercial spaces and office buildings is provided by direct steam provided by the local utility, Con Edison. Cooling systems are commonly powered by electricity, although gas and other fossil fuels are sometimes employed.

At Audubon House, heating and cooling are provided almost exclusively by a single source: a gas-fired chiller-heater located on the top floor. This energy-efficient machine and the choice of natural gas to run it set Audubon House apart from conventional buildings and embody the goals and principles of the project. The chiller-heater is both literally and figuratively the heart of Audubon House, driving its circulatory system and reducing its environmental impact. The architects had contemplated a similar system for their NRDC renovation, but correctly sized equipment was not available then. By buying and thoroughly renovating its new headquarters, Audubon could consider the full range of options for its heating and cooling needs.

Fully installed York gas-fired absorption chiller-heater at Audubon House. This high-efficiency heater-chiller runs on a six-step chilling cycle and a three-step heating cycle. The tight thermal insulation and efficient lighting at Audubon House resulted in the downsizing of this equipment by almost half. The choice of natural gas fuel had major implications for Audubon's environmental goals, which are discussed in this chapter. (© Jeff Goldberg/Esto.)

The advantages of on-site heating and cooling provided by a gas-fired chiller-heater system over other systems are discussed in detail later. Among the most immediate and obvious: The chiller-heater does not contribute to emissions of sulfur oxides and reduces the contribution of nitrogen oxides. In addition, it produces no emissions of chlorofluorocarbons (CFCs) because it uses lithium bromide and water rather than conventional refrigerants in the cooling cycle. The on-site burning of gas is generally more efficient than most other on-site energy sources (under specific regional conditions) and avoids most of the environmental problems associated with oil, coal, and nuclear energy. Equally important, the gas-fired chiller-heater will save Audubon roughly $18,000 a year in demand charges over an electrical system that operates off the electricity "grid," based on the DOE-2 energy simulation model.

Description of the System

The chiller-heater at Audubon House has a cooling capacity of 180 tons and a heating capacity of of 1.7 million Btu per hour. It is known as an "absorption" chiller-heater, which refers to its operation, shown in the accompanying diagram. The three-step heating cycle heats water that is circulated through pipes along the perimeter of the building on each floor. The six-step cooling cycle produces chilled water that circulates through air-handler cooling coils that cool the air on each floor. Fans circulate air over the chilled-water cooling coils, cooling and dehumidifying the air before directing it to the occupied offices. The unit itself can be fueled with either oil or gas; Audubon chose natural gas.

Utility companies are realizing the opportunities for avoided costs and optimizing their systems through energy reduction and fuels strategies. We see more people—building owners as well as utility executives—becoming advocates for integrated high-performance design.

RANDOLPH CROXTON

To understand the full benefits of Audubon's heating and cooling system, one must not only look at the chiller-heater but at the HVAC system as a whole. Several important features of the system add significantly to the building's overall efficiency and the thermal comfort of its occupants. Separate controls that regulate the flow of hot water through the pipes are located in several strate-

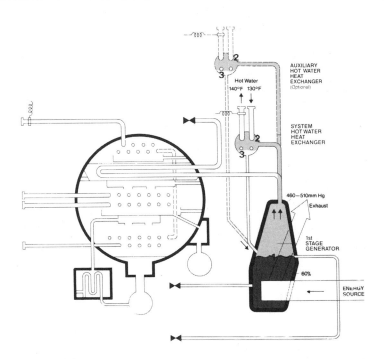

AUXILIARY
HOT WATER
HEAT
EXCHANGER
(Optional)

Hot Water
140°F 130°F

SYSTEM
HOT WATER
HEAT
EXCHANGER

460—510mm Hg

Exhaust

1st
STAGE
GENERATOR

60%

ENERGY
SOURCE

Schematic diagram of the heating cycle. (Courtesy of York International Corporation.)

gic locations on each floor, giving employees greater control over individual climate and potentially saving energy that would be lost to overheating.

The cooling and ventilation system at Audubon House does not rely on a central air distribution unit, but rather on individual fan rooms containing air-handling units at each floor. Highly filtered outdoor air enters the building at the roof (it is warmed during winter), then is distributed directly to fan rooms, where it is mixed with recirculated return air from each floor. Fans at each floor draw air through cooling coils containing chilled water and distribute the air through ductwork to air terminal outlets. These outlets have temperature-sensing devices (variable air volume controls, or VAVs), which modulate the air volume passing through each outlet in response to space temperature. The amount of air can also be modulated by a fan using a static pressure sensor mounted in the ductwork and a variable frequency drive that electronically slows the fan motor, which reduces energy significantly, yet maintains comfort.

Each VAV outlet is its own controlled temperature

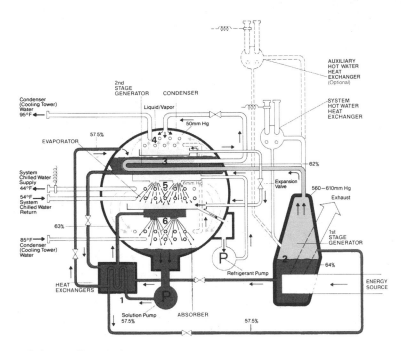

Schematic diagram of the cooling cycle.

1. First a dilute solution of lithium bromide and water descends from the absorber to the solution pump. This flow of dilute solution is split into two streams and pumped through heat exchangers to the first- and second-stage generators.

2. *First-stage generator:* An energy source heats dilute lithium bromide solution coming from the solution pump/heat exchangers. This produces hot refrigerant vapor, which is sent to the second-stage generator, leaving a concentrated solution that is returned to the heat exchangers.

3. *Second-stage generator:* The energy source from the production of refrigerant vapor in the second-stage generator is the hot refrigerant vapor produced by the first-stage generator. This additional refrigerant vapor is produced when dilute solution from the heat exchanger is heated by refrigerant vapor from the first-stage generator. The additional concentrated solution that results is returned to the heat exchanger. The refrigerant vapor from the first-stage generator condenses into liquid, giving up its heat, and continues to the condenser.

4. *Condenser:* Refrigerant from two sources—(1) liquid resulting from the condensing of vapor produced in the first-stage generator, and (2) vapor produced by the second-stage generator—enters the condenser. The refrigerant vapor is condensed into liquid and the refrigerant liquid is cooled. The refrigerant liquids are combined and cooled by the condenser water. The liquid then flows to the bottom of the evaporator through a U

trap, which separates the higher condenser pressure from the low evaporator pressure.

5. *Evaporator* (chilling effect): Refrigerant flows down to the refrigerant pump, where it is pumped up to the top of the evaporator. Here the liquid is sprayed out as a fine mist over the evaporator tubes. Due to the extreme vacuum in the evaporator, some of the refrigerant liquid vaporizes, creating the refrigerant effect. (This vacuum is created by hygroscopic action—the strong affinity lithium bromide has for water—in the absorber directly adjacent.) The refrigeration effect cools returning system chilled water in the evaporator tubes. The refrigerant liquid/vapor picks up the heat of the returning chilled water, cooling it from 54°F to 44°F. The chilled water is then supplied back to the system.

6. *Absorber:* As refrigerant vapor travels to the absorber from the evaporator, concentrated solution coming from the heat exchanger is sprayed out into the flow of refrigerant vapor. The hygroscopic action between lithium bromide and water and temperature result in the creation of an extreme vacuum in the evaporator directly adjacent. The dissolving of the lithium bromide water gives off heat, which is removed by condenser water entering from the cooling tower at 85°F and leaving the condenser at 95°F. The resultant dilute lithium bromide solution collects in the bottom of the absorber, where it flows down to the solution pump. The chilling cycle is now complete. (Courtesy of York International Corporation.)

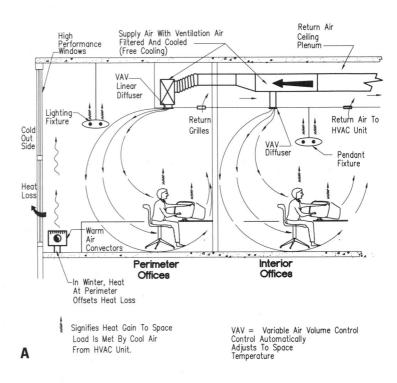

A

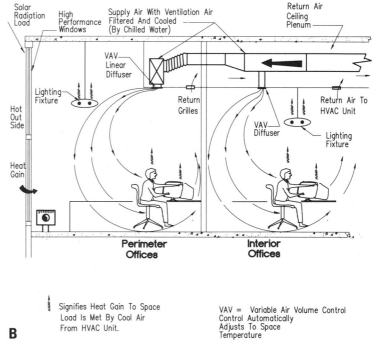

Cross section of a typical work area, showing features that enhance thermal comfort.

a. In colder months, hot water flows to fin-tube convectors located at the building's perimeter. Warm air rising from the convector acts as a "curtain" to block colder air along the windows and wall.

b. In warmer months, chilled water flows to cooling coils in the airhandling rooms on each floor. There fresh air and recirculated air mixed and cooled. Variable air volume (VAV) outlets conduct the air into office spaces; each VAV box is fitted with adjustable temperature-control diffusers, allowing a high-degree of individual thermal comfort.

B

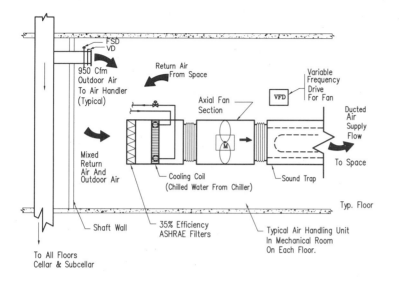

Diagram of an air-handling unit. Each floor at Audubon House has its own air-handling room. Here, outdoor and recirculated air are mixed and refiltered. Variable speed drives on the unit fans adjust fan speed according to a pre-set static pressure point—an energy-saving feature. (Courtesy of Flack + Kurtz.)

Variable air volume (VAV) outlet. Located at regular intervals in the ceilings, these boxes conduct air from the air handling rooms to the interior space. Each has a Thermafuser™ to adjust temperature within a pre-set range, allowing each employee a high degree of control over personal comfort.

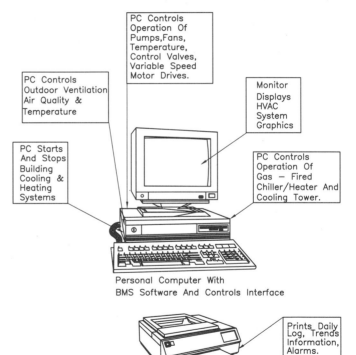

PC Controls
Outdoor Ventilation
Air Quality &
Temperature

PC Controls
Operation Of
Pumps,Fans,
Temperature,
Control Valves,
Variable Speed
Motor Drives.

Monitor
Displays
HVAC
System
Graphics

PC Starts
And Stops
Building
Cooling &
Heating
Systems

PC Controls
Operation Of
Gas — Fired
Chiller/Heater And
Cooling Tower.

Personal Computer With
BMS Software And Controls Interface

Prints Daily
Log, Trends
Information,
Alarms.

Laser Printer

Computerized building management system at Audubon House:
    a. the building manager's computer command center, 7th floor;
    b. diagram of the system.
The building manager can adjust temperatures on individual floors,
and the system can automatically choose from among three cooling
options, saving substantially on energy. (Photo by Tom Mead, draw-
ing courtesy of Flack + Kurtz.)

zone and gives each office and workspace better temperature comfort for individual needs. In addition, each
floor is equipped with a temperature sensor to monitor
overall comfort. Temperature readings are relayed to a
central computer, which in turn can control the absorption chiller, further reducing energy demand.

Audubon House has been equipped with two supplemental systems that at moderate temperatures draw
nighttime air from outdoors directly into the offices, pre-

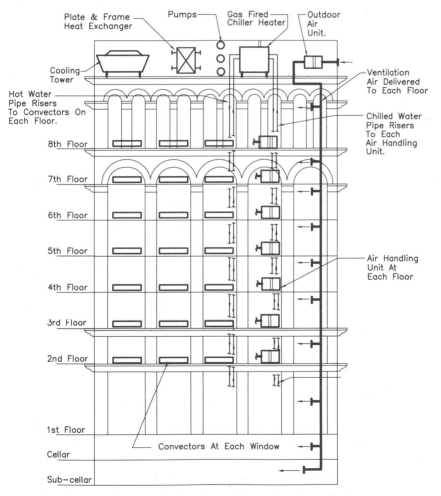

*Audubon House—diagram of elevation with overlay of ventilation
system. A high fresh air ratio and high-performance filters ensure
that indoor air quality will exceed standards. (Courtesy of Flack +
Kurtz.)*

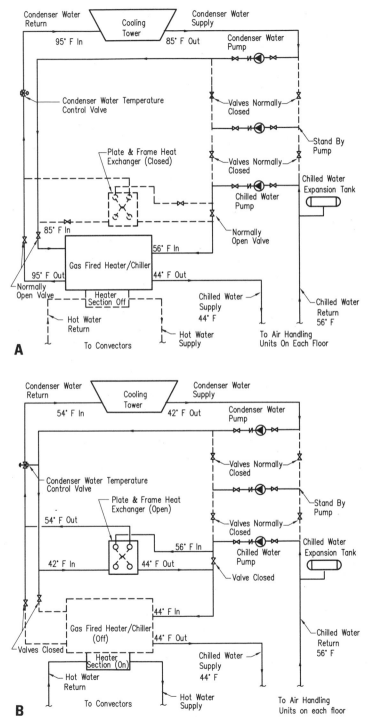

Diagram showing integrated cooling (a) and heating (b) systems at Audubon House. In both cases, most heating and cooling are supplied by the gas-fired absorption chiller-heated located on the rooftop (ninth) floor.

a. During warmer months, fresh air is drawn into the building at the rooftop level and passed to individual air-handling rooms on each floor, where it is mixed with recirculated air and passed over coils cooled with chilled water from the chiller. In more temperate conditions, an economizer cycle or cool air can substitute for the chiller.

b. During colder months, fresh air is warmed after intake and then passes to the air handling rooms. Additional warming is supplied by hot water distributed to perimeter fin-tube convectors. (Courtesy of Flack + Kurtz.)

cooling the building and saving energy. The building's system can also be operated on an economizer cycle, whereby the water is chilled by direct temperature exchange with water from the cooling tower. At moderate outdoor temperatures (40 to 55°F) use of the economizer cycle totally eliminates the need for operating the absorption chiller. It is worth noting that although Audubon does not employ "active" solar energy (photovoltaic cells) in this scheme, both supplemental systems meet the definition of "passive" solar energy applications.

Using the central computer system, the building operator's computer can interactively select the least energy-intensive system or combination of systems for a given situation. Thus although there are more advanced HVAC systems on the market, Audubon's is certainly a finely tuned, "smart" system. It can respond to individual needs and adjust to provide optimal comfort conditions. More important, in its use of passive solar alternatives that require little energy input, it is a partially *nature-driven,* rather than an *energy-driven,* system. Audubon's nature-driven system adjusts automatically to minor variations of temperature outdoors as well as indoors, providing the optimum environmental conditions while saving significant amounts of energy.

Economics of the System

When Audubon purchased the absorption chiller-heater for its new headquarters, it cost $102,000 more than the most advanced electric cooling system available, after a $72,000 conservation rebate for the equipment from Con Edison. As noted earlier, the chiller-heater saves $18,000 in electricity costs. In addition, the compactness of the system saved Audubon space in the building, worth roughly $15,000 in savings. Based on these estimates, the simple payback for the chiller-heater alone is in the range of three to five years. Additional savings of about $10,000 are generated by the overall HVAC system, including the variable speed fans, variable air valve boxes, and other features.

As with much of the technology and alternative materials they purchased for Audubon House, the project leaders hoped that the acquisition of the chiller-heater would stimulate the market for similar machinery. If so, prices can be expected to decline, spurring builders to buy similar technology and further stimulating the markets. Indeed, this may be already happening with the gas-fired absorption technology. Audubon's unit was manufactured in Japan and distributed in the United States. When Audubon bought the unit, there were no domestic manufacturers. Since then, at least one U.S. firm is manufacturing absorption chiller-heaters and two more have opened distributorships.

Choosing Gas: Environmental Considerations

The choice of fuel for heating and cooling systems is challenging. One has to rely as much on professional judgment as on scientific analysis. The number of factors to be weighed against one another is extensive and varies from one site to the next. Energy markets and sources vary from region to region and from year to year, making evaluation of environmental impacts difficult. While natural gas was found to be the appropriate choice for Audubon House, it may not necessarily be so for other projects and under different circumstances.

Audubon was aided in the selection process by the DOE-2 computer program, which allowed the team to compare the overall energy savings of the system to conventional code-compliant models while taking into account the building's energy-efficient design features. DOE-2 helped confirm the energy-saving potential of using the gas-fired chiller-heater equipment.

Both during and after the installation of the chiller-heater, the Audubon Team endeavored to analyze the comparative environmental benefits and drawbacks of gas as an energy source. The results of this analysis are summarized on the following pages. Rather than indicating a "correct" outcome, this analysis suggests a general method by which builders may begin to make their own determination of an appropriate fuel choice.

An Energy Source for Heating: Electricity, Oil, or Gas?

From the start, the choice of gas as the source of heating was never seriously in doubt. Audubon's location in the Northeast, where winters are cold, made the use of electricity impractical. In this region, although electricity is low in installation costs, it is an expensive source of energy for heat, even in a well-insulated building. In some parts of the country, such as the South, where utility rates are lower and heating requirements less, electricity may be preferable. A more serious contender at Audubon House was fuel oil, a common source of heating in many offices and residential dwellings in the Northeast.

The combination of advanced technology and energy-efficient design modifications at Audubon House has created an environment in which the mechanical system operates almost like a high-performance sports car: It has the ability to respond to changing environmental conditions with great speed and accuracy. The heating and cooling performance of the building as a whole has exceeded our expectations. It's more than just an energy-efficient building.

JORDAN FOX

An evaluation of the heavy environmental impacts of oil extraction and associated activities seemed to favor gas strongly. Oil drilling is a massive industrial process that has despoiled many natural areas. In some states, open pits where waste oil and its by-products are stored have created a hazard for birds and wildlife. Despite domestic laws calling for double-hulled tankers, response teams, and other measures, oil spills large and small continue to exact an enormous environmental toll worldwide. Environmentally sensitive areas such as the Arctic National Wildlife Refuge in Alaska—the protection of which is a top priority for Audubon—are under attack for their supposed oil supplies. And the United States' increasing dependence on foreign oil has become a volatile and divisive national security issue.

The team also had to take into account the relative pollution caused by burning gas as opposed to burning oil. When compared to No. 2 fuel oil over a 30-year period, gas was clearly the cleaner-burning fuel. The burning of gas emits 70 percent less nitric oxide, 38 percent less carbon dioxide, and 16 percent less carbon monoxide does than the burning of fuel.

An Energy Source for Cooling: Gas or Electricity?

Two electrical cooling systems were considered: individual cooling units on each floor, and a central centrifugal chiller. An advantage of electrical cooling is its greater on-site efficiency, measured by "coefficient of performance" (COP)—the quantity of heat energy removed from the building, or "cooling," for each unit of energy input. Table 5.1 shows the COP of gas versus the two electrical systems, with a higher COP meaning greater efficiency. On this basis, electric would appear to be the better choice. However, other factors require consideration as well.

We tend to forget that electricity is more than what is on the other side of the light switch. Nationwide, hundreds of coal and oil plants, nuclear reactors, hydroelectric dams, and other sources generate the electricity that

TABLE 5.1. Coefficient of Performance and Relative Energy Inputs of Gas Chiller Versus Two Different Electric Chillers[a]

	Electric I	Electric II	Gas
Cooling COP gas			1.1
Cooling COP electricity	3.3	5	
Electrical loss factor	3.3	3.3	
Heat energy removed	1	1	1
Energy input to chiller	0.33	0.2	1
Energy input at utility	1.1	0.66	NA
Total energy required	1.1	0.66	1

[a] *Electric I, individual floor-packaged units; electric II, central centrifugal chiller; gas, gas-fired chiller.*

feeds the grids that power our cities—and the buildings in them. Each utility uses a particular source, or mixture of sources, to provide its customers with electricity. At the time of the Audubon House renovation, Con Edison, the local utility, used the following mixture:

- 36 percent oil
- 26 percent nuclear
- 22 percent natural gas
- 10 percent hydroelectric
- 5 percent coal
- 1 percent waste (methane, biomass, etc.)

Con Edison also imports electric power from the New York Power Pool (NYPP), which is generated from the same kinds of energy sources.

Thus the Audubon Team's calculations had to take into account the relative environmental impacts of *each* of these sources as compared to on-site gas. Table 5.2 represents a general environmental accounting for the relative impacts of these various sources. Coal was seen as the biggest environmental liability. It is easily the most polluting of fossil fuels, a major contributor to acid rain and global warming. Although it was a small portion of Con Edison's mix, nationwide it accounts for an average of 57 percent of utility electricity, and the Audubon Team felt that it had to consider the broader implications of this source. The superiority of gas over oil in terms of emissions has already been noted.

Nuclear energy was similarly problematic. The dis-

TABLE 5.2. Direct Environmental Impacts from Utility Sources

	Gas	Oil	Coal	Nuclear	Hydro
Nuclear waste				High	
Sulfur Oxides (acid rain)	Very low	Medium	High		
Nitrogen oxides (acid rain)	Medium	Medium	Medium		
Carbon dioxide (global warming)	Low	Medium	High		
Lost habitat	Low	Medium	Medium	Low	High

Note: Where no value is given, it is assumed to be negligible.

posal of nuclear waste remains an unsolved dilemma, as does the issue of safety. Waste energy generated by incinerators, although a minuscule part of the mix, presents the benefit of recapturing resources rather than using new ones. But incinerators pose controversial social as well as environmental issues. They often emit pollutants—sometimes toxic—and communities tend to view them as undesirable.

Hydroelectric power makes perhaps the best case for use of electricity over gas, especially when existing dams are used. Hydropower is virtually nonpolluting and theoretically renewable. But the construction of new dams results in widespread environmental destruction, often of ecologically vital habitats; potentially reduces water flows in rivers; and indirectly at least can contribute to global warming by the removal of trees, which collect carbon dioxide.

At this stage, the team used a value judgment based on Audubon's environmental priorities: the society has opposed plans by the Canadian utility Hydro-Quebec to build a massive new series of dams in the James Bay region of Canada. Some Northeastern states, including New York, have considered importing power from Hydro-Quebec. Rejecting hydropower was an important confirmation of Audubon's view that James Bay should be protected from the devastation of new dams.

As a final step, the Audubon team weighed the approximate cumulative impacts of electricity, based on the mix of sources at the time, for both proposed electric systems and for gas. (In addition, a "best-case" scenario for future electricity generation was compared, using the assumption that all electricity will ultimately be generated by gas burned in low-polluting "combined cycle" units that are now coming into use. This gives some idea of how Audubon House will perform comparatively when the rest of the world "catches up.") The results of these estimates are depicted as a "decision matrix" (Table 5.3). This table compares Audubon House to the best-performing electric system (Electric II) and to the best-case future scenario. Emissions from the New York Power Pool were used in the decision matrix because they are well documented and correspond to the elec-

TABLE 5.3. Decision Matrix for Audubon House Energy Source: Relative Pollution Loading (Relative Units) for Gas Absorption Chiller versus Electric II (Central Centrifugal Chiller) versus Best-Case Future Scenario in Which Utility Burns Natural Gas in a Combined-Cycle Unit

	Electric II[a]	Gas Chiller	Best-Case Future—Electric[b]
Nitrogen oxides	3.7	1	1.1
Carbon dioxide	1.2	1	0.6
Carbon monoxide	3.7	1	0.66
Sulfur oxides	5.2	0.01	0.004
Total suspended particulates	1.7	0.1	0.02
Volatile organic compounds	0.3	1	4
CFCs	1	0	0
Nuclear waste	1	0	0
Habitat loss	1	Approx. 0	Approx. 0

[a] New York Power Pool, summer peak.
[b] Combined-cycle gas-combustion unit.

tricity Con Edison imports. The results should generally reflect the impacts from the fuels that Con Edison uses at its own facilities.[35]

In all but one of the nine categories shown, gas performed better than the Electricity II scenario assuming the current utility energy mix. Even in the hypothetical best-case future utility scenario, on-site gas did better than or equal to electricity in four of the nine categories. As time goes on, the utility mix will shift from the high-emissions case closer to the combined-cycle case, but will be unlikely to reach it over the next 30 years because utilities will probably retain some of their inefficient, highly polluting units. Except in the category of carbon dioxide emissions, a comparison of the cumulative emissions projected over the next 30 years favors on-site gas.[36]

[35] Data for states other than New York for the three major fossil fuel pollutants can be found in Procurement Guide for *Renewable Energy Systems: A Handbook for State and Local Governments,* Interstate Renewable Energy Council, 1993. Available from the New York State Energy Office, Albany, N.Y.
[36] Basic emissions data used to construct the tables have been taken from a report prepared by the Tellus Institute of Boston for a study, "Environmental Impacts of Long Island's Energy Choices," *Tellus Project 90-028A,* Sept. 1990, Tables 4 and 5. We assume that the emissions data given by Tellus for "natural gas commercial space heat" match emissions from Audubon's gas absorption chiller.

When seen in combination with the highly insulated thermal shell at Audubon House, the choice of gas looks even better. In Table 5.4 we compare the environmental impacts of using on-site gas as Audubon House to the estimated impacts of electricity in a ctnventional code-compliant building of comparable size using Electric II and also to the best-case future electric utility scenario. Here, gas far outperforms both electric models.

Choosing gas over electricity had one additional bene-fit—it drastically lowered Audubon's need for electricity in the summertime. This reduction of peak demand lessens the strain on already overburdened utilities to supply peak-season power and eases the pressure to develop new energy sources. By cutting its peak demand, Audubon was able to win substantial rebates from Con Edison.

Other Options

Three other alternatives were considered briefly. Steam energy from a utility may in some places be a feasible choice but was prohibitively expensive for Audubon. A different gas chiller-heater, called a gas screw compressor, scored lower on coefficient of performance. Solar energy, of course, was highly desirable, being the most en-

TABLE 5.4. Conventional Code-Compliant Building with Electric Chiller versus Audubon House, Fully Insulated, with Gas (Relative Units).

	Electric II[a]	Gas Chiller	Best-Case Future—Electric[b]
Nitrogen oxides	9.3	1	2.8
Carbon dioxide	3	1	1.5
Carbon monoxide	9.1	1	1.7
Sulfur oxides	13	0.01	0.009
Total suspended particulates	4.2	0.1	0.05
Volatile organic compounds	0.7	1	10
CFCs	2.4	0	0
Nuclear waste	2.4	0	0
Habitat loss	2.4	Approx. 0	Approx. 0

[a] *New York Power Pool, summer peak.*
[b] *Combined-cycle gas-combustion unit.*

vironmentally benign energy source. Audubon looked closely at putting a panel of solar photovoltaic cells, which convert sunlight directly to electricity, on the rooftop. Unfortunately, photovoltaic (PV) systems did not meet the three to five-year payback requirement. But the architects did complete initial solar energy studies to support their eventual installation should they become cost-effective. In addition, Audubon House uses passive solar energy in its two supplemental cooling systems—night cooling and an economizer cycle—and, most directly, in the daylighting of the building.

The choice of gas for heating and cooling Audubon House is a real-world solution to a difficult problem. Any energy source carries an environmental price, even so-called renewable energy sources. Rather than waiting for technology to come up with the "perfect" energy source—an illusory goal in any event—Audubon House shows how energy efficiency acquired through existing "smart" technology and simple design modifications can dramatically reduce a building's impact on the global environment. Through a combination of energy and resource conservation and recycling strategies, over the lifetime of the building Audubon House is assured of leaving a smaller "footprint" than its neighbors.

The Healthy Workplace: Ventilation and Materials

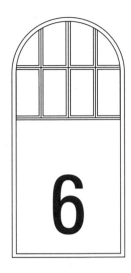

6

A T LEAST A FEW participants in the official dedication of Audubon House may have observed an anomaly. Walking into the building's ground-floor lobby, they would have seen workers putting the finishing touches to the paint job. But they would not have smelled anything. The paint that was used here and for most of the building's walls and ceilings had no detectable odor—a tip-off to another, more important fact— that it was virtually free of harmful volatile organic compounds (VOCs). The use of this odor-free, nontoxic paint symbolizes the Audubon Team's commitment to creating a healthy indoor environment for the 170 employees of Audubon House.

Two major components contribute to poor indoor air quality. One is merely code compliant ventilation and filtration combined with a poorly designed HVAC distribution system. This can intensify one or more of the following: the increase in levels of unhealthy pollutants in the air; development and transmission of molds, bacteria, and other toxins through air ducts; and "stale" air that has not been changed or lacks a sufficient ratio of outdoor ("fresh") air. The other is the buildup of toxic compounds in the air emitted, or off-gassed, from common building materials, products, and especially finishes. Most of these compounds, including formaldehyde and solvents such as benzene, toluene, and xylene, are called *volatile organic compounds,* or VOCs, and are found in such building products as carpeting, glues, furniture, paints, and tiles. They are generally emitted into the air, or off-gassed, over many years, although sanding or other maintenance may increase the rate of offgassing. Such compounds may sometimes cause short-term health effects or discomfort. Of greater concern, however, are the risks of long-term exposure to these compounds, which may include cancer, developmental defects, immune system disorders, and other health problems.

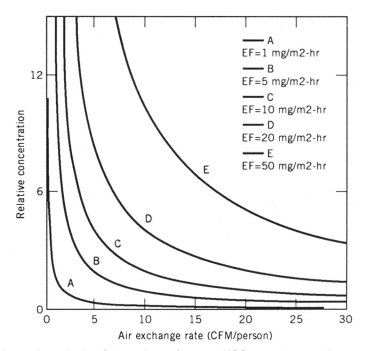

Rate of ventilation (air exchange) versus VOC source strength, shown as an inverse relationship. In a typical building, the higher the rate of air exchange with the outside air and the weaker the sources of volatile organic compounds (VOCs), the lower the overall concentration of VOCs will be. Audubon House addressed the issue from both ends, minimizing the installation of materials with VOC content and establishing a high rate of air exchange (26 cfm/person). Thus Audubon House is expected to be an extremely healthy indoor environment.

The Audubon Team employed strategies to combat poor air quality on both these fronts. The HVAC system contains a number of features that boost the freshness and cleanliness of the indoor air well above code-compliant levels and reduce the likelihood of exposure to bacteria and other contaminants. Many of these features have been well known to building professionals for many years.

By comparison, the strategy pursued by the designer and environmental expert—identifying and purchasing nontoxic or low-toxic alternatives to conventional building materials and products—is a more recent one, and consequently more complicated and difficult. The rewards were great, however; in some instances, it led to the novel applications of available materials. This kind of flexible, creative approach was essential in an area where surprisingly little systematic and thorough information exists. The results of these efforts to create a healthier indoor environment were immediately evident in the noticeable freshness of the indoor air at Audubon House. More detailed corroboration will have to await long-term studies but can be expected to show a marked improvement in indoor air quality and a corollary increase in worker productivity.

Ventilation

Sometimes seemingly simple adjustments make the biggest difference. At Audubon's old headquarters, the "fresh" air intake vent was located near ground level, right over the building's loading dock, where exhaust fumes from idling trucks and automobiles would be most concentrated. This is not an uncommon occurrence among existing office buildings; intake vents are frequently placed at street level, where pollution is highest, or abutting exhaust vents, the latter circumstance creating a compromised air source. Air drawn in from such a location can hardly be called "fresh."

At Audubon House, the intake vent is located on the southern exposure (the most open side of the building)

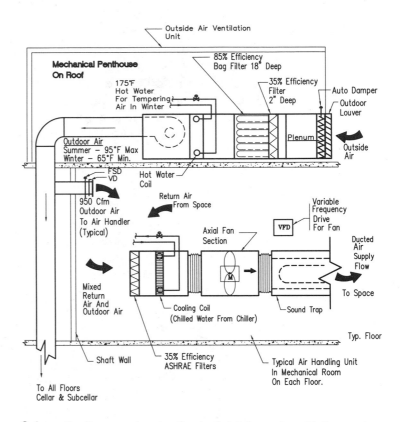

Schematic diagram showing fresh-air intake and ventilation system. Note that the fresh air is filtered twice—initially with a high-efficiency bag filter (ASHRAE 85%) and again on each exchange. (Courtesy of Flack + Kurtz.)

of the rooftop level, where it is far from street level. This placement ensures that the cleanest available air is brought in from the start. The intake vent is fitted with a grill to filter out the largest particulates, and an overhead rain-guard "eave" minimizes moisture entering the system. Audubon House also delivers *more* outdoor air to each occupant than standard office buildings—a constant 26 cubic feet per minute (cfm) per person (which can go as high as 30 cfm). The American Society of Heating, Refrigerating, and Air-Conditioning Engineers (ASHRAE), the body that sets professional standards relating to indoor air quality and ventilation, recommends 20 cfm per person. Many existing offices provide 10 cfm or less.

The outdoor air is drawn through a highly efficient bag filter that removes a high proportion of particles and other pollutants from the air. This filter is rated at 85 percent efficiency by ASHRAE; compared to the typical filter of 35 percent efficiency, the filter used at Audubon captures significantly more pollutants.[37] The higher-efficiency filter also reduces odors (except from gases), and the cleaner air prolongs the life of HVAC components. The disadvantages are minimal: This filter has a 3 to 5% higher first cost, uses slightly more energy (the fan must work harder to draw the air), and requires more frequent maintenance.

The placement of fresh air intake vents is one of those things engineers take for granted—with unfortunate results. I have seen plenty of intake vents built over loading docks or right next to the exhaust. At Audubon House, we considered not only the placement of the intake vent but also protecting it from moisture and nearby pollution. As a result, we get the freshest air possible.

JORDAN FOX

The filtered outdoor air then goes directly to the air-handling rooms on each floor (described in Chapter 5), where it mixes with recirculated air. The mixed air is further filtered on each "pass" through the handling room, with an ASHRAE-rated 35 percent efficiency filter. In effect, the outdoor air is filtered twice. Air changes take place an average of 6.3 times an hour, more than three times as often as the ASHRAE standard (2 times an hour) at the time of the renovation and 35 percent more

---

[37] ASHRAE assesses air-filter efficiency using an "atmospheric dust spot test." Fine dust particles are blown through a filter onto a clean piece of paper over a given period of time, and the resulting proportion of "dust spots" that hit the paper determines the rating. A high-efficiency filter will allow many fewer and finer particles to get through. U.S. EPA and NIOSH, *Building Air Quality: A Guide for Building Owners and Facility Managers* (Dec. 1991).

often than is called for in the current standard (4 times an hour). More frequent air changes help reduce the buildup of toxins and minimizes the potential for stale air pockets to occur.

Specially designed ventilation ducts that have greater capacity than conventional ducts, along with the use of low-speed fans to conduct the air, help take moisture out of the circulating air, thus reducing the potential for the growth of biological contaminants and their distribution into the air. The system is well designed for easy maintenance and cleaning.

Air intake vent, rooftop level; bag filter for fresh air. Because it is located on the rooftop level and away from the exhaust, the fresh air intake at Audubon House draws the freshest available air. The grill filters large particulates and an overhanging eaves minimizes moisture intake. Inside, the fresh air passes through a high-efficiency (ASHRAE 85 percent) bag filter. (Photo by Tom Mead.)

Although quantitative measurements are not yet available, there is no doubt that the combination of high-performance strategies and components used in every aspect of the ventilation system at Audubon House produce exceptionally high indoor air quality. As well as providing for the health of the building occupants, these features—along with the individually adjustable variable air volume outlets used throughout and adjustable temperature controls for heating and cooling—add immeasurably to employees' comfort and well-being.

Material Choices

More than any aspect of the Audubon project, the process of purchasing materials and products for the building challenged the team with a complex array of choices and factors. Before describing the individual components used at Audubon House, this process deserves some explication. Some readers may choose to study this section closely for its applicability to other projects.

First, there was the possibility of competing criteria. What was more important? The product's impact on indoor air quality? Upstream environmental impacts from the manufacture of the product? Or downstream environmental impacts from its use and disposal? Compared to the upstream and downstream impacts, indoor air quality generally affects the client more directly; also, information on chemical composition was usually more readily available than data on manufacturing processes or disposal, making predictions of indoor air quality impacts more reliable. As a result, the Audubon Team decided to give first priority to indoor air quality, followed by downstream impacts and, last, upstream impacts.

When the team could identify egregious trade-offs in terms of upstream or downstream impacts, however, it made sense to make an exception. (*Exception* is the watchword of environmental decision making—the key is flexibility, not rigid rule making!) For example, polyvinyl chloride plastic (PVC) emits highly toxic compounds when incinerated (a potential outcome of its disposal).

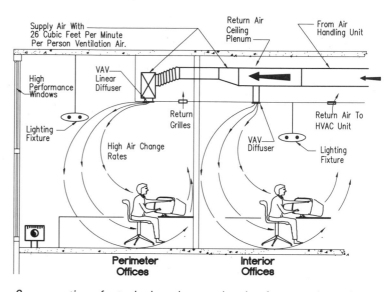

Cross section of a typical work area showing features that enhance indoor air quality. Increased frequency of variable air volume outlets in the ceiling creates improved air mixing and flow at Audubon House, helping to prevent the build-up of "stale air" pockets.

Thus it was avoided whenever possible. Similarly, where the use of pressed wood was indicated, the team had a choice of one product made with low-toxic glues and sawdust from California redwoods or another made with a different sawdust but a less environmentally clean glue. Because the Audubon Society places a premium concern on biodiversity and the protection of habitats (including primary forests), the team chose the latter product.

In addition to direct and indirect environmental impacts of each product, the team looked at criteria such as embodied energy, the overall environmental policies of manufacturers, health and safety conditions at their factories, and even social responsibility. The product's performance, economy, comfort, and aesthetics were primary considerations as well. In some cases, the performance of a product under certain conditions made its selection difficult. In the corner of the building where the pantries were designed, for example, water had rotted out the original wooden flooring, so the team installed plywood subflooring with a conventional tile covering instead of preferable alternatives. However, all such plywood was specified to be exterior grade, which is made with phenol formaldehyde—an adhesive that does not off-gas at room temperature.

Items such as furniture and carpeting had to be aesthetically pleasing and comfortable for occupants as well as environmentally acceptable. In selecting fabric for the workstation partitions, for instance, the interior designer substituted a different material than the manufacturer's on aesthetic grounds. Although this fabric had good environmental characteristics, it had not been independently tested for emissions of formaldehyde and VOCs. The team required that the manufacturer confirm in writing that no formaldehyde was used in the fabric's manufacture.

The selection of materials presented the opportunity for the team to advance the "recycling" objectives of the project by purchasing items made of recycled or recyclable materials. Some consideration was also given to "natural" materials, with the understanding that such materials do not *necessarily* have less of an environmental impact than "synthetic" products. Finally, the design of customized wood furnishings for conference rooms offered the unique opportunity to encourage sustainable forestry practices.

Assessing Chemicals

Suppose that two somewhat similar products existed for the same purpose—for instance, plastic laminate for workspace partitions. How could the Audubon Team make the environmentally better choice? The issue is not a simple one. Ideally, it would be possible to assess exactly the environmental *risk* of every chemical component, by knowing precisely the quantity of the chemical involved, how easily it is off-gassed and transmitted to people, and the probability that a given unit of concentration will produce side effects. Current realities generally place such a procedure beyond the capacity of environmental experts or designers. (A noticeable exception at Audubon House was the workstations, where manufacturer's data on the rate of off-gassing of formaldehyde allowed the team to estimate air concentrations of the gas over time, and thus calculate risk.)

Instead, the team relied on material safety data sheets (MSDS) to establish the presence or absence of harmful chemicals in products. (See Appendix C for a sample MSDS.) These sheets list the names and amounts of any substances *in* a product that pose a potential risk. If any were listed, the environmental expert checked them further against a scientific list of cancer-causing compounds (IARC list of carcinongens, see Appendix J) or, if necessary, consulted a toxicology handbook. Thus the analysis of two or more products' MSDS sheets could often establish which product was least likely to be deleterious to the indoor air quality and to have the least overall negative environmental effects.

When the environmental advantages of one product over another were minimal, I would agree to purchase the less expensive product. This gave me a degree of flexibility to argue for products with clearly superior environmental advantages even when they cost substantially more.

JAN BEYEA

The team supplemented the information from MSDS sheets with data from manufacturers on product composition and other relevant factors, when such data were made available. A lack of information from some manufacturers influenced certain decisions, notably the choice of carpeting. Sometimes, too, the team had to utilize generic research on products and materials, or simply broad strategies to avoid harmful substances. Examples of the latter include avoiding or minimizing adhesives and pressed wood, which contain formaldehyde and VOCs, and objects that had a "new car" smell—an indication that these and other toxic compounds existed in the material.

Generic research played a key role in the comparison of plastic products to paper products (Beyea, Audubon's chief scientist, is a recognized expert on paper/plastic comparison) and to each other. Widely available research on various plastics allowed the environmental expert to rank them on a pound-for-pound basis, as follows:

Polyethelene, polypropylene: benign
- *PET and polystyrene:* intermediate
- *ABS:* questionable
- *Polyvinyl chloride (PVC):* to be avoided whenever possible

Products Used at Audubon House: Selected Examples

Floors. At an early stage in the project, the architects determined that a "subfloor" layer would have to be placed over the original, damaged floors. Conventional subflooring is most commonly made of interior-grade plywood—thin layers of wood bonded with urea-formaldehyde. The Audubon Team wanted to avoid materials that would off-gas formaldehyde, but finding an alternative was not easy, because few had been tried in office buildings.

The architect and designer suggested using Homasote™, a material made of recycled newsprint (50 percent by weight) pressed and bound with a low-toxic bonding agent (0.9. paraffin wax) and a low-toxic fire-retardant (aluminum hydrate). This material had been used primarily in residential construction as a sound-absorbing floor surface; prior large-scale commercial applications were few. After the architect, at the insistence of the owner's representative, undertook the research necessary to establish that the product had been used successfully, the Homasote™ subflooring was installed. The contractors encountered difficulties during the initial installation, with some sections buckling as a result of the natural acclimation to moisture, but reinstallation corrected the problem. The material eventually withstood a

Homasote™, stacked prior to installation as subflooring. This material, made primarily of recycled newsprint pressed and bound with a low-toxic bonding agent, was used as subflooring in a large-scale office building for the first time at Audubon House. Conventional subflooring made of plywood is a source of formaldehyde and VOCs. The use of Homasote™ exemplifies the Audubon Team's commitment to high indoor air quality and the use of recycled materials. (Courtesy of Bernstein Associates.)

year of unprotected use during construction, a source of relief to Audubon, and it has held up well to date.

Carpeting. For the carpet underlayer, the team identified a natural product—an "old-fashioned" jute-hair pad—to replace conventional synthetic pads, frequently a source of formaldehyde, benzene, toluene, and other toxins. Jute is a plant fiber, which is then blended with natural hair from cattle; the resulting "felted" material is coated with a rubberized outer layer to form the pad.

The carpet itself is also a natural product: 100 percent wool, woven "Wilton" in a basketweave pattern of three colors, from three breeds of sheep. It uses no dyes; the manufacture of dyes has significant upstream environmental impacts, particularly water pollution caused by waste products. The wool was scoured with biodegrad-

Wool carpeting at Audubon House. The use of all-natural, undyed wool carpeting illustrates the team's use of natural products as well as to reducing VOC emissions. In addition, the carpeting was tacked down without glues (except on the staircases), further reducing potential sources of VOCs. (© Jeff Goldberg/Esto.)

able detergents instead of with conventional phosphates or other polluting detergents. To minimize the use of adhesives, the carpeting was laid directly over the jute-hair pad and tacked down (except on staircases, for safety reasons).

Although use of domestically produced goods is usually preferable (partly because it avoids long-distance transportation), the carpeting Audubon purchased was imported from the Netherlands. European mills had more experience and could provide baseline information on the environmental performance of their products and manufacturing processes, whereas American manufacturers could not.

As with any products, there are drawbacks to the natural wool carpet. While the process of creating a wool carpet is generally more environmentally benign than manufacturing a synthetic one, sheep farming and other aspects of the process are not without impacts. Some question has also arisen about the tendency of wool carpeting under normal circumstances to absorb volatile organic compounds (VOCs) in the daytime and during cleaning, releasing them into the indoor air after hours. However, Audubon House differs from a typical installation because it has a very low VOC load to begin with, and the carpet will not be "shampooed" with cleansers containing solvents and other toxins. Therefore, the carpet is not expected to cause indoor air quality problems. An additional plus is that the processing of wool fiber uses much less energy than manufacturing synthetic fibers from petrochemicals.

Drywall. In place of standard gypsum plasterboard, the Audubon Team installed wallboard that consists of a partially recycled gypsum core with outer layers of 100 percent recycled paper. The team considered a second brand that had a higher percentage of recycled gypsum, but the manufacturer of the chosen brand had a better in-house record of recycling water and reusing energy. (One hundred percent recycled newsprint treated with a fire-retardant salt solution was also used as fire-safing in the construction of Audubon House).

Paint. Finding interior paints that satisfied Audubon's criteria was among the most daunting challenges facing the team. The complexity was due to the range of paints needed (five different "qualities" for different surfaces) and the numerous chemical constituents of paints, which include pigments, brighteners, fillers, preservatives (biocides), drying agents, and solvents. The team solicited information on these constituents from MSDS sheets and other data supplied by manufacturers, comparing named compounds against the IARC list of carcinogens, list of hazardous materials published by the Occupational Safety and Health Administration (OSHA), and toxicology handbooks.

Several alternatives were initially specified by the design team in the contract documents, but all posed problems. One line of paints was made with a base of natural plant pigments and oils, making it desirable from an environmental viewpoint, but it was prohibitively expensive, so it was used only in small areas as a test. Two lines of latex paints were compared: one was found to have a number of hazardous substances; the other appeared to contain no unacceptable pigments or additives, and the manufacturer reported low VOCs (added to make paint fast-drying), low biocides (biocides inhibit microbial growth and increase shelf life), and only trace amounts of crystalline silica (a constituent of most paints which, when airborne, can cause pulmonary fibrosis).

A legislated standard for a product or product assembly may not be the right one to target. You might have to create your own standards for acceptable thresholds of pollutants in materials. It is also important to look for anomalies in the test results of products—for instance, if emissions increase over the test period (despite initial testing results conforming to your chosen threshhold). Here may be reason to investigate the product further to determine the source of the increase.

KIRSTEN CHILDS

The team was prepared to use this paint, but the contractors were dissatisfied with the credit terms offered by its manufacturer and proposed yet another alternative. MSDS sheets revealed that four of the five paints in the line suggested by the contractors had small amounts of crystalline silica and higher VOC emissions than the team's preferred paints, and the fifth contained a potential carcinogen. In the meantime, however, the team's preferred alternative was deemed to be too expensive. At this impasse, yet another line of paints came on the market that did not off-gas VOCs and had an acceptable chemical composition. This paint was offered at a reasonable price, and because of its superior environmental performance, the team purchased it. In the absence of VOC emissions, this paint gave off no detectable odor during its application.

Furniture. Whenever possible, the team avoided pressed wood furniture, which can be a major source of off-gassing. Chairs are made from aluminum or steel with low-toxic fabrics and with foam made without CFCs and containing no toluene. Rubberized components were substituted for components made of PVC plastic. Recycled materials were also incorporated: the workstation shelving is made partially from recycled steel and the bathroom countertops are made with recycled PET plastic from discarded containers.

The efforts of the team to verify data on formaldehyhde emissions of the furniture resulted in some intriguing discoveries. As noted earlier, such data do exist; a standard 30-day "chamber" test is administered from which air concentrations of formaldehyde can be measured. Looking at the test results for the furniture preferred by the designer, the team discovered an unusual occurrence: the emissions of formaldehyde had actually increased during the test period, instead of decreasing as is normal. This suggested that over time, the formaldehyde emissions would exceed acceptable standards. When the anomaly was pointed out to the manufacturer, the manufacturer undertook research to pinpoint the source of the problem: the desktop had a heavily glued "honeycomb" core, from which it was surmised that the formaldehyde slowly seeped through pre-drilled screw holes. The manufacturer was then able to offer an environmentally better alternative. Although Audubon eventually purchased a lower-cost line of furniture (with acceptable air-quality standards), this episode illustrates the benefits of cooperation between environmentalists and manufacturers willing to develop better products.

Audubon House has four small corner conference rooms on floors four through seven and a large central conference room for staff meetings on the eighth floor. The tables and cabinets in these rooms are visually

Reception desk, eighth floor. Customized wood furniture at Audubon House is made with sustainably harvested rainforest mahogany certified by the New York–based Rainforest Alliance. The purchase of such products is intended to encourage the sustainable use of rainforest resources, ultimately aiding in conservation efforts. (Photo by Tom Mead.)

among the most striking elements in the building. They are also a visible symbol of Audubon's commitment to one of the most urgent environmental issues of the day, the preservation of forests. The conference tables and cabinets were custom designed for Audubon House using *sustainably* grown North American cherry and mahogany from tropical rainforests. The mahogany was purchased through the "Smart Wood" program of the New York–based Rainforest Alliance, which certifies only wood that is grown sustainably. The purchase of sustainable rainforest products encourages the adoption of sustainable practices by rainforest peoples, which it is hoped will put the brakes on unsustainable exploitation of these irreplaceable treasures.

Adhesives. Although the team sought to minimize or avoid the use of adhesives throughout the project—for example, tacking the carpeting in place instead of gluing it—the use of glues is unavoidable and indeed ubiquitous in any building. When the use of glues was dictated at Audubon House, the team looked at MSDS sheets and selected environmentally superior products. On the advice of the environmental expert, the team avoided glues made with phenol compounds. These compounds are federally listed as hazardous substances and wastes and may be released into the water during manufacture, potentially contaminating fish and other life.

No choice is perfect. We have to find the best possible solution under the circumstances, and any analysis depends on site-specific considerations.
JAN BEYEA

In selecting an adhesive for the tiles in the pantries, the team looked at three different products. All three contained VOCs, but no alternative was known that would still perform adequately and maintain the manufacturer's guarantee. The environmental expert ultimately chose the product that used naturally occurring VOCs instead of manufactured ones, inferring that the former would be less harmful.

The Audubon Team's strategy for selecting products has the advantage that it will tend to drive manufacturers in the right direction, toward ever "greener" products. Future project leaders will find the task of finding environmentally sound products increasingly easy. The American Institute of Architects *Environmental Resource Guide,* of which only a few sections were available during the Audubon project, now lists many environmentally sound products and manufacturers. The guide uses Audubon House as its first case study in environmental design.

As with other facets of the Audubon project, there was a premium cost, or added "first cost," involved in purchasing environmentally friendly products and materials. Although the payback cannot be measured in concrete terms, it is nevertheless substantial; a healthy workplace is no longer a luxury but an essential part of doing business. Audubon House proves that by strategically shifting costs—for instance by reducing expenditures for high-end finishes, handrails, paneling, and such—it is possible to stay within the original budget cost and market-rate targets for any given project.

Recycling at Audubon: Closing the Loop

T HE SAME YEAR that Audubon purchased its new headquarters, New York City faced a serious solid waste crisis. It still does. In 1989, the city disposed of more than 19,000 tons of trash each day. Nearly three fourths of this garbage, or 12,000 tons, was dumped into a single landfill—Fresh Kills on Staten Island, the largest landfill in the world. Fresh Kills has been operating in violation of state pollution laws for years and will reach its capacity sometime early in the next century. Another 2,395 tons per day of the Big Apple's garbage was burned in incinerators, creating untold air pollution problems. Only 1,250 tons per day, a mere .65. percent, was recovered through recycling programs. Bottle and can returns resulting from the state's bottle deposit law, which places a 5-cent returnable deposit on retail beverage containers, represented more than a third of the recovery rate.[38]

Little has changed today in New York. The city government remains firmly committed to constructing a new series of municipal incinerators to handle some of the burgeoning trash, a solution bitterly opposed by environmentalists who warn of unresolved issues from disposal

---

[38] Source of solid waste figures: Eric A. Goldstein and Mark A. Izeman (Natural Resources Defense Council), *The New York Environment Book* (Washington, D.C.: Island Press, 1990).

Fresh Kills landfill, Staten Island, New York City. This mountain of trash has come to symbolize the growing garbage crisis in New York City and nationwide. One of only two operating landfills left in the city, Fresh Kills will reach capacity sometime in the next five to ten years. The five-point recycling program at Audubon House points the way for commercial buildings to help solve the crisis today. (Courtesy of New York City Department of Sanitation.)

of hazardous ash and air pollution. And similar problems beset communities around the country. The best municipal recycling efforts, like those of Seattle and Newark, recover up to 50 percent of the municipal waste stream, but these are the exception. Nationwide, the amount of garbage grows every year. In 1991, a whopping 280 million tons of waste was generated, of which 75 percent ended up in landfills, 10 percent was incinerated, and only 14 percent was recycled.[39]

---

[39] World Resources Institute, *1993 Information Please Environmental Almanac.*

Not all of the picture is so bleak. For example, 6.6 million tons of old newsprint was recycled in 1991 in the United States, an increase of 90 percent from 1983, contributing to a total of 31.1 million tons of paper recycled.[40] Nevertheless, efforts at recycling have been hampered by a number of factors, including slow markets for recycleable materials and the difficulty in changing people's habits.

Against this backdrop, the Audubon Team sought to make recycling a centerpiece of Audubon House. The goal was to set up a model office solid waste program that would alleviate Audubon's direct contribution to the waste stream and, more important, set a reasonable standard for others to emulate. By setting an example, the team also hoped to spur other establishments to recycle and thus to stimulate local recycling markets.

Audubon's solid waste program includes both recycling components and those that limit the consumption of resources. It can be broken into five broad areas:

1. "Recycling" the building: renovating an existing structure
2. Recycling materials from demolition
3. Finding building materials made with recycled content
4. Programming and designing a physical in-house recycling system to capture office waste
5. Establishing guidelines for the purchase of recycled and/or recyclable supplies (as well as waste reduction and reuse)

Of these, perhaps the most far-reaching is the development of an comprehensive, building-wide recycling system, the goal of which is to capture nearly 80 percent of the society's office waste, including 42 tons of paper annually. A similar system employed in offices throughout the country could save the equivalent of 30 million trees a year.

Implementation of a building-wide recycling system was made feasible by Audubon's owning the building,

---

[40] Ibid.

allowing the architects to progress beyond the constraints of their earlier work at NRDC; however, building ownership is not a necessary condition to instituting a thorough office recycling system, nor was it a factor in the four other major components of Audubon's program.

Recycling the Building

By purchasing a standing building instead of building a new one, Audubon right away made a strong statement in support of saving resources and energy. The "recycling" of 700 Broadway resulted in the preservation of approximately 300 tons of steel, 9,000 tons of masonry, and 560 tons of concrete. Had the building been demolished, under a conventional contract these materials might well have ended up in landfills. Further, construction of a new office building of comparable size would have required the extraction and/or manufacture of material, with the attendant drain on natural resources and energy, and environmental impacts (although some of this could be offset by the purchase of recycled building materials, as Audubon did for its interior reconstruction). The preservation of an existing building thus not only represented a conservation of material but also embodied energy.

Beyond the direct environmental benefits, reuse of an existing structure amounted to a gesture of respect toward the community. Instead of imposing a new aesthetic on an architecturally rich section of New York City, Audubon conserved a building of great character and an integral piece of the overall architectural fabric. (In the area where Audubon House is located can be found some of the earliest examples of cast-iron building and works by such early Modern masters as Louis Sullivan, Post, and others.)

Last, but not least, the society also saved money. It is estimated that construction of a conventional new building on the same site would have cost $17 to $18 million; with purchase of the site and demolition, the total cost could have been more than a third higher than the $24 million Audubon paid for the purchase and reuse of 700 Broadway.[41]

In the spirit of the environmental directive to "reduce, reuse, and recycle," the Audubon Society chose to reuse an existing building, saving money, energy, and resources and promoting an environmental approach at a basic level of decision making. Corporate executives and other decision makers considering relocation would be well advised to consider renovation, retrofitting, and other alternatives to new construction whenever feasible.

Recycling Demolished Materials

Although Audubon would have chosen, if possible, to put every scrap of the old building to use, the renovation inevitably required demolition and removal of existing material and its replacement by new construction. Accordingly, the Audubon Team placed a high priority on finding vendors to recycle gutted building materials, stipulating in writing that the subcontractor sort the materials, separate them for shipment to recyclers, and identify recycling vendors.

For two materials, recycling was eliminated as an option: window glass, because at the time no nearby vendor could be found, making the cost of shipment prohibitive; and heating oil. The oil, which had spilled onto the ground from the original boiler in the subbasement, was found to be contaminated with mercury, and so was disposed of appropriately as hazardous waste. The balance of materials from demolition was recycled successfully. Iron, tin, and steel—including the old boiler itself—were sold to a scrap metal dealer. Wood from window frames and the original rooftop water tower was sent to a vendor in Brooklyn to be used for garden landscaping materials.

---

[41] It is difficult to make more than a very rough comparison between the Audubon project and a hypothetical new building on the same site. Audubon House has a much greater floor-to-ceiling height than a modern building as well as radically different construction. Zoning changes have also lowered the legal height of new building in the location of Audubon House.

Used concrete and masonry was sent out to be crushed into roadbed fill.

Recycling for many of these materials is still in its infancy, and only the metals "broke even" on a balance sheet; the other materials had an associated recycling cost. However, the cost of recycling was *less* than Audubon would otherwise have paid for dumping. As markets expand for recyclables, it is likely that in the near future recycling building materials will turn a profit for owners.

Demolition material from Audubon House sorted for recycling. As part of their work agreement, the demolition subcontractors were required to arrange for the recycling of masonry, concrete, metal, and other material removed from Audubon House. With the exception of glass and oil, most of the material was recycled successfully. (Photo by Otto Baitz.)

Recycled Building Materials

Using materials made with recycled content has several benefits: It reduces the amount of new materials required and thus the consumption of energy and natural resources, it diverts materials from the waste stream, and it stimulates the market for recycled goods, thereby having a salutary effect on recycling efforts as a whole.

The average office worker throws away 100 pounds of paper every year. If you consider all office workers in the country, this amounts to an estimated 30 million trees. Our landfills—where plastics, metals, and other office waste are buried—are stretched to the limit. Yet a number of construction and office products made of reconstituted materials are now on the market, and their widespread use would go a long way towards conserving resources and alleviating the crisis in solid-waste disposal.

JAN BEYEA

Environmentalists put particular emphasis on the recycling of "postconsumer" materials—those that have passed into the hands of consumers. Such materials make up the bulk of what is disposed of in landfills and incinerators. Paradoxically, they are the most difficult and therefore often the last to be recycled. Reprocessing postconsumer wastes often requires more equipment and infrastructure than do preconsumer wastes. For example, postconsumer waste paper must be deinked and rid of impurities before it can be reused in most paper grades. Thus the need for developing markets for postconsumer materials is greatest.

The Audubon Team used recycled building materials whenever they were readily available and economically feasible. Some examples are:

- Bathroom countertops made with a high-density polymer resin compound, part of which comes from recycled postconsumer plastic—actually used deter-

Bathroom countertops. Whenever it was feasible, the Audubon Team purchased recycled building materials, preferably those that had reached the end use ("postconsumer"). These countertops are made with recycled plastic from used detergent bottles and their kin. (Photo by Tom Mead.)

Floor tiles and their main material: light bulbs. These tiles, made in part of recycled waste glass from the manufacture of light bulbs, were installed for demonstration purposes in the ground-floor lobby and elevator vestibules at Audubon House. (Courtesy of Croxton Collaborative Architects.)

gent bottles and their kin. Because of this product's cost, the Audubon Team chose to limit its installation to bathroom countertops only, although the product is also available for bathroom partitions, tabletops, and other uses.

- Floor tiles in the elevator vestibules made of 60 percent preconsumer recycled glass (waste from incandescent light bulb manufacturing), in place of conventional vinyl or ceramic tile. Although these priced out at a higher level than was deemed most economical, they were purchased to demonstrate this new use for a "waste" material.

- Gypsum wallboard for dividing offices made with a partially recycled gypsum core (8 to 15%) and outer layers of 100 percent recycled paper. A similar product with a higher content of recycled gypsum was

Ground-floor entryway and lobby. Decorative tiles made of recycled glass welcome visitors to Audubon House. (Courtesy of Bernstein Associates.)

considered but was rejected on the basis of the manufacturer's less favorable record of water recycling and energy reuse.

- Partially recycled steel studs for construction; 25 percent recycled steel for library and workstation shelving; partially recycled aluminum in furniture frames. The furniture is also designed specifically so that it can be returned to the manufacturer for recycling.
- Homasote™ subflooring (see previous chapter).
- Fireproofing made from recycled newsprint.

Although some of these products require an added monetary investment, increased commercial and residential use of such products should bring prices down steadily in the future. However, public pressure must also be put on policymakers to adopt higher standards for recycled products in building codes and product requirements.

In-house Recycling System

The centerpiece of Audubon's recycling program is a comprehensive, building-wide recycling system that when fully operational will recycle about 80 percent of the society's office waste. With advice and a grant from Waste Management, Inc. the architect designed a series of chutes to take sorted materials for recycling and a basement recycling room. Audubon's environmental scientists added a desktop recycling system for individual offices and are monitoring the daily operation of the recycling program.

The cost of the recycling system added about $185,000 to the renovation cost, but it is still included in the overall market-rate cost of $122 per square foot. For Audubon, the cost was insignificant next to the current and future benefits. Audubon's recycling program symbolizes the society's commitment to solid waste issues and environmental progress. Moreover, in coming years, local, state, and federal laws and regulations are likely to be adopted requiring greater recycling efforts on the part of commercial establishments. With its thorough recycling system, Audubon has a "jump-start" on other businesses as well as a hedge against future costs. In addition, the growth of recycling markets is likely to produce revenues from the sale of recyclable materials, so that it is not inconceivable that Audubon's system could pay for itself within a decade or less.

Preparations for the recycling system actually began in 1991 at Audubon's old midtown headquarters, where employees were subjected to the Audubon "Garbage Test." Over a single week, employees were required to sort their refuse into 12 categories, ranging from food waste and white paper to glass and appliances. The science staff placed bins in all the hallways to collect the sorted trash. At the end of the week, the scientists placed the trash in separate bags and weighed them to determine the total amount accumulated in each category. (See Appendix H for detailed instructions on administering the test.)

The results of the two-week study are shown in Table 7.1. They are fairly typical of an office, with paper prod-

TABLE 7.1. Results of the Audubon Garbage Test

Category	Percent
Hazardous materials	0.3
Newspapers	13.7
Magazines, glossy brochures	13.7
White office paper	31.6
Mixed paper	9.3
Other paper	7.2
Shiny cardboard	0.1
Corrugated cardboard	4.0
Compostables	4.1
Mixed materials	1.8
Plastics	1.9
Glass, cans, metals	4.7
Electrical or heavy equipment	0.2
Miscellaneous	7.5

Total pounds discarded: 1,135. Note that all paper products add up to approximately 80 percent.

ucts composing more than four-fifths of the waste stream. A total of 1,135 pounds of garbage was discarded during the week, or 227 pounds a day, averaging out to 1.8 pounds per person per day. (By this measure, the average person discards at least twice their body weight every year in paper alone!)

Further analysis showed that Audubon already recycled 35 percent of its trash—white paper (including office paper) and "redeemable" beverage containers, which by New York state law can be returned to vendors in exchange for a 5-cent deposit. It was estimated that recycling newspapers would increase the figure to 50 percent; adding in mixed and coated papers would raise it to 73 percent; cardboard, to 77 percent; and food scraps and soiled paper, to 80 percent. Thus Audubon set a realistic goal of recycling 80 percent of its solid waste.

The Garbage Test not only provided Audubon with valuable data to plan a recycling program, it also taught em-

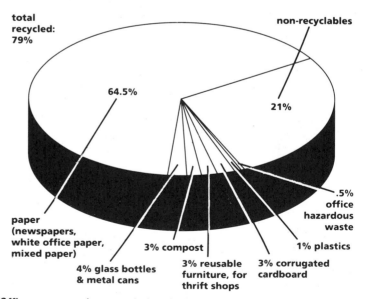

Office waste to be recycled at Audubon House. An analysis of office waste at Audubon undertaken in 1991 confirmed that close to 80 percent of it could be recycled. That is the target set for Audubon's ambitious in-house recycling program.

ployees to recognize the various types of materials, that many items are made of combinations of materials, and not to take their disposal lightly. In effect, it created the beginnings of a recycling ethic in employees; cooperation of individual participants is critical to the success of the program. Said one employee, "Taking the test made me think about both ends of the spectrum: where garbage originates and where it ends up. Does a store-bought sandwich have to be double-wrapped in foil? Can I use the back of a letter as scrap paper? The test made a lot of us realize we weren't doing nearly enough to reduce our waste stream."

Recycling Chutes and Collection Room

To achieve its recycling goal, Audubon had to devise a system that was user-friendly for employees and centralized for easy collection and processing. For these reasons, the architects constructed a system of four recycling chutes running through the building's entire elevation (see the accompanying diagram). The 20-inch steel chutes are similar to garbage disposal chutes found in apartment buildings. Pull-back doors give employees and other building occupants access to the chutes on every floor. As a fire-safety measure, an interlocking system of electrical sensors prevents more than one door of each chute from being opened at the same time.

Each chute is designated for a different material. One is located in the vestibule for copying machines and is for white and computer paper. Three are located in the pantries and are for mixed paper (colored paper, file folders, paperboard, and Post-it notes), redeemable aluminum cans and plastic bottles (those covered under the state deposit law), and food wastes. In addition to the chutes, shelves were constructed in the corner of each kitchen for the collection of materials. Initially, these have been used to collect newspapers, magazines and coated papers, and redeemable glass bottles, with other categories expected to be added later. Materials on the shelves are picked up by building maintenance staff,

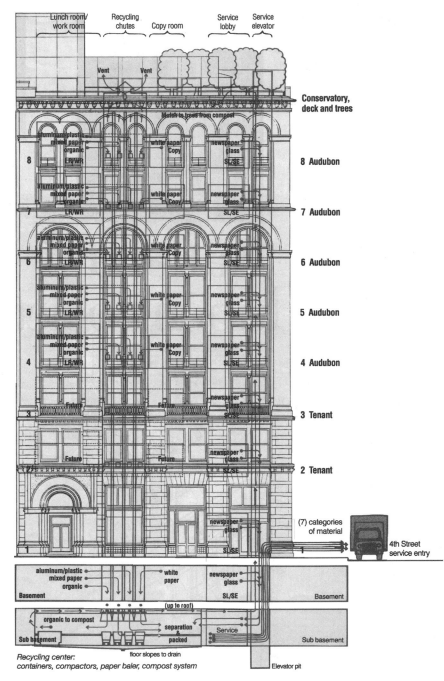

Audubon House, sketch of elevation showing recycling system. Four recycling chutes, one each for white office paper, mixed paper, organic wastes, and plastic beverage containers, run the entire elevation of the building. (Courtesy of Croxton Collaborative, Architects.)

Recycling chutes under construction. Four chutes run the length of the building from the eighth floor to the sub-basement recycling room. (Photo by Otto Baitz.)

while employees are responsible for dumping those materials earmarked for the chutes.

Each employee was given two "waste baskets," one to collect mixed paper and the other for unrecycled garbage, and two desktop trays, one for paper to be reused by the employee and one for white paper to be recycled. In addition to encouraging employees to reuse paper before recycling it—an important first step in any solid waste reduction program—the desktop and office recycling units facilitate the sorting of recyclables and their transport to the chutes. Appropriately, the baskets and trays are made of recycled plastics.

Pantry recycling area. Employees are responsible for bringing their sorted wastes to one of four recycling chutes (the fourth is not shown). Some materials, such as glass and newspapers, are picked up from pantry shelves and brought to the subbasement recycling room. (© Jeff Goldberg/Esto.)

The recycling chutes empty into large, movable collection bins inside a specially designed recycling room in the building's subbasement. The building maintenance staff picks up recyclables stacked on the pantry shelves and brings them to the recycling room as well. From there, the materials are taken the short distance to the building's delivery entrance, where they are picked up by the appropriate recycler.

The recycling room is the most important component of the overall recycling system, as well as the most unique. By installing sprinklers and carefully arranging the room's layout, the Audubon Team allowed the room

Subbasement recycling room. Ample storage space and the installation of separate sprinklers make this an ideal recycling room. To meet the inevitable advent of stricter recycling laws, building owners who install operable recycling facilities like these will save time and money over those who lag behind. (Photo by Tom Mead.)

to be used for storage of large quantities of paper and other recyclables, without violating fire safety rules and other building codes. The likelihood of increasingly strict recycling laws making the recycling of greater quantities of material mandatory will undoubtedly require owners of commercial establishments to build similar recycling rooms. Owners would be well advised to take the first opportunity (the programming phase of new projects) to do so rather than waiting until a costly retrofit is needed.

To achieve the best results with maximum cooperation of employees, Audubon is implementing the recycling program in stages. Audubon science staff is providing the leadership for implementation of the program. After a year, Audubon was already recycling a substantial percentage of its office waste (exact figures were not available at the time of printing). White office paper and computer paper, mixed paper, newspapers, magazines, and coated (glossy) paper were all being picked up by a private recycler. Redeemable beverage containers were being taken by a local nonprofit company called We Can, which gives the revenue from the nickel deposit on beverage containers to homeless men and women as well as employing them throughout the company. Recycling for other materials—nonredeemable containers, glass, plastic, and metal—as well as composting for food wastes was anticipated to be in place by mid-1994, bringing the total of recycled materials close to the 80 percent target.

During the first year of the recycling program, Audubon was making a nominal "profit" from the recycling of white office paper. Other materials were recycled at a

Employee's waste baskets. All employees at Audubon House received two "waste" baskets for separating garbage from mixed paper, as well as two desktop trays for accumulating white paper and reusable paper, in order to facilitate the presorting of recyclables. Employee education and cooperation are critical to the success of any office recycling program. (Photo by Tom Mead.)

slight loss, but garbage carting fees were reduced. Once Audubon's recycling program is fully implemented and captures most of the office waste materials, Audubon, as a nonprofit organization, will qualify for New York City's residential recycling program. With the city picking up all of Audubon's recyclables and trash, the society will then be saving more than $12,000 a year. In cases where this option is not possible, however, building owners will still find recycling to be a less costly option than garbage hauling. As the value of recyclable materials increases, recycling may eventually turn a profit for businesses.

A small percentage of Audubon's office waste contains hazardous materials. Based on the Garbage Test, Audubon scientists estimated that Audubon discards at most 200 pounds a year of hazardous waste, including such items as toner cartridges from copiers and laser printers (about 90 cartridges a year), burned-out fluorescent lamps (although Audubon's high-efficiency lamps have a longer life expectancy than that of conventional bulbs), batteries, "liquid paper," and cleansers. As part of its guidelines for purchasing office products (see below), Audubon management is encouraging employees and maintenance staff to reduce their use of these products or to find low-toxic or recycled substitutes when possible. Many such goods, such as rechargeable batteries and low-toxic cleansers, are readily available on the market. Waste Management has to cart away the remaining hazardous waste for proper disposal.

Composting

Experimental on-site composting is expected to be phased in at Audubon sometime in 1994. Composting at Audubon House is one of the most promising and unique aspects of the recycling effort. If the composting experiment succeeds, it will bear out the feasibility of composting in an office-building environment. In preparation for its implementation at Audubon House, various composting models are being tested at Scully Science Center, an Audubon facility on Long Island.

To initiate the program, small or easily broken down food scraps and soft soiled paper will be collected via the recycling chutes or by maintenance staff. In the recycling room, the food waste will be held in refrigerators. When enough has accumulated, the waste will be passed through a grate, to remove large, difficult-to-compost solids, into one of four composting vessels. Each enclosed plastic vessel, or composting reactor, has a 40-pound capacity. The use of enclosed vessels is critical to minimizing potential odors from the decaying material—an essential criterion in the success of the project.

Audubon adheres to a 10 percent limit in cost premiums for individual green purchases of office supplies, but that does not mean that total purchasing costs will rise by that much. Not every alternative costs more. We don't expect more than a 2 to 3 percent increase in the cost of office supplies.
JAMES CUNNINGHAM, CHIEF FINANCIAL OFFICER,
NATIONAL AUDUBON SOCIETY

Audubon plans to use an aerobic composting system, which involves supplying a steady flow of air to the reactors, promoting the growth of bacteria that break down the waste. Each reactor will be separately ventilated; the exhaust will pass through a biofilter to removed potential toxins and odors. Aerobic composting—the same kind of composting that is done in backyards—is faster and more odor-free than anaerobic composting.

The aerobic process can be approximately divided into two stages. To begin the composting process, compost "starter" (initially, compost purchased from a garden store; later, Audubon will be able to start the process with its own compost) and wood chips are added to the food waste, as well as air and water to bring the temperature to approximately 140°F. The reactors are enclosed with insulation to maintain the desired temperature. If necessary, some fertilizer may be added to provide nitrogen. After a minimum of three days at this temperature, the contents of the waste are sterilized. In this first stage, much of the waste decomposes rapidly.

In the second stage, the compost is "cured" in the reactors. That is, over a period of about three months, the smaller organic particles slowly turn into a rich humus, or compost. Less active management is needed in this stage. At the end of the process, the finished compost will be transported to planters on the building's rooftop.

Purchasing Guidelines

Like employees in any business, Audubon staff must be provided with supplies and equipment to carry out their work, including stationery and computer equipment as well as more mundane items such as pencils and paper clips. Audubon is in the process of setting up guidelines for the purchase of office supplies and equipment. These guidelines will mandate or encourage employees to reduce their consumption of, or buy environmentally sound, supplies and materials. The following are examples of what employees would be asked to do under such guidelines:

1. Purchase products with a high degree of recycled content, preferably postconsumer. An overall goal would be the purchase of at least as much recycled material as waste collected for recycling at Audubon, in order to help stimulate recycling markets.
2. Whenever possible, purchase recycled paper that has not been bleached. Chlorine bleaching releases dioxins, a suspected human carcinogen.
3. Use rebuilt cartridges for laser printers and copying machines, or buy laser printers that do not require cartridge replacement.
4. For large purchases, develop a certification process that takes into account the full life-cycle impacts of the materials involved.
5. Avoid the purchase of mixed-material goods such as paper and plastic combinations, unless the component materials can be separated easily. Mixed materials are generally harder to recycle.
6. Use grease pencils instead of felt markers, which emit VOCs.

In keeping with the economic imperative of the project, Audubon has set a 10 percent limit on cost premiums for "green" purchases. Given the rapidly declining prices of such items, however, an increase of no more than 1 to 2 percent in office supply expenditures is expected.

A large proportion of Audubon's work involves publishing and disseminating information to educate members and the public. Audubon publishes a bimonthly magazine, *Audubon*, read by more than a million people; a quarterly magazine, *American Birds*; a monthly news journal, *Audubon Activist*; a children's newspaper, *Audubon Adventures*; and various fact sheets, brochures, and other publications. The society also sends out numerous membership and fund-raising mailings. Audubon is in the midst of an organization-wide analysis of its mailings and publications that will result in standards to reduce their environmental impacts. Already, most of them are printed on recycled paper, using soy-based rather than petroleum-based inks. Other steps that will be considered at Audubon include elimination of "glassine" windows in envelopes and the use of papers with higher postconsumer content.

Finally, guidelines will be propagated to encourage employees to reduce their contribution to waste and promote environmental habits. Simple measures, such as reusing paper that has only one used side, double-sided copying, circulating memos rather than making multiple copies, refusing excessive packaging when shopping for lunch, and bringing a reusable coffee mug and dishes, can take a significant bite out of the total office waste stream.

Office Maintenance

It is important to remember that all the components of Audubon's waste-reduction and recycling program will be applicable to other tenants (including retail operations) throughout the building. As an added measure, building maintenance operations will also be aligned with the goals of the program. For example, purchasing guidelines will also be promulgated for cleaning and planting supplies (Audubon's offices include plants arranged in selected areas of the floors).

Audubon spent many months experimenting with carpet cleaning mixtures to find the one least harmful to the environment. Conventional cleaners made with ammonia or isopropyl alcohol give off VOCs and have significant upstream impacts, but Audubon couldn't use steam cleaning either, because the wool carpeting does not take it well. After trying more than 10 mixtures, Audubon found a mild soap that removes loose dirt but was still looking for a benign formula for removing stains.

Similarly, Audubon has conducted ongoing experiments to find an environmentally sound cleaning process for removing graffiti from the building facade. At least one cleanser had listed propylene glycol monomethyl ether (PGME) as an ingredient, which is listed in toxicology handbooks as an irritant and central nervous system depressant, potentially a hazard for workers using it. Its use was preferred over a product with a potential carcinogen but was avoided in favor of a product with no hazardous chemicals at all.

Once the "wave of the future," reducing waste at the source and recycling have become the wave of the present—the best and, indeed, the only real way out of our growing solid waste crisis. More than it has in any other area, Audubon House, with its building-wide recycling program, has set a precedent for "green living." Like the other features of the Audubon project, the recycling program requires little in the way of extra financial investment, but it represents a worthwhile investment of intellectual effort, creativity, and commitment to environmental principles. Its success can be measured not only in the palpable reduction of trash in employees' waste baskets but also in the enthusiastic support it has received from everyone inside Audubon House.

Conclusion: A Success in the Making

8

I T HAS BEEN a year since the National Audubon Society moved into its new headquarters at 700 Broadway. And people are still talking about it. Audubon employees, especially those who worked in the decidedly unpleasant environment of Audubon's previous headquarters, frequently remark on the pleasant ambience of Audubon House. Visitors, too, usually express surprise and delight at the light, airy feeling of the interior, so distinct from the crammed, stuffy feeling found in so many office buildings. With the exterior of Audubon House newly restored and adorned by the banner of the National Audubon Society, people strolling by on a typi-

---

I love coming here to work every day. I love knowing that I'm not breathing crud. In the other building I'd look up at the air vents and they were always full of grime. Maintenance people were in here cleaning the vents just yesterday. I like to see that. I like the building so much that I give tours. It's very sunny, very visually appealing. I like working in an open area rather than an enclosed space. I like how accessible people are here.

ELIZABETH HAX, EXECUTIVE SECRETARY, MEMBERSHIP DEPARTMENT, NATIONAL AUDUBON SOCIETY

A living model: Audubon House today, from the corner of Broadway and 4th Street. Audubon's environmentally sound and energy-efficient headquarters has become a fixture in lower Manhattan and attracts visitors from around the world. It truly exemplifies the environmental motto: Think Globally, Act Locally. (© Jeff Goldberg/ Esto.)

cal day stop to gaze up and admire the classical architecture and welcome the "new kid on the block."

Audubon House has received a steady stream of visitors from around the world, eager to see and learn about the principles put into practice by the Audubon Team and to take them back to their communities. They have included high-powered business leaders and politicians, distinguished architects, engineers, designers, environmental educators, activists, and people from nearly every other walk of life. Many of them have been actively involved in ongoing or planned building projects and have come to learn about specific systems or to get design ideas. Some have entered with the notion that Audubon House is an expensive technological wonder—a collection of high-efficiency gadgets, state-of-the-art "superwindows," and so on. These people have had their

---

I did not like the old building. There was a perfume manufacturer on another floor and sometimes the odors coming through the air system were enough to drive you out of your office. The building did a lousy job of providing an even temperature in summer and winter. People constantly had heaters out in winter, and fans in summer. And between the stillness of the air and the flickering lights, by 4 p.m. every day I was dragging. It's nice not to deal with those problems any more. At Audubon House I'm in the office at 8 a.m. and I stay until 7 p.m. And I still have a little extra energy at the end of the day. I think the air is so much better here, and there is greater productivity. Everyone is enthusiastic about what we've accomplished. When you invite friends here, they say, 'Wow, this place looks great!' Sometimes it just stretches their imagination.

JAMES A. CUNNINGHAM

---

eyes opened when they learn about the Audubon approach—and then hear the project's competitive, market-rate price tag. Others have come just to see what the shape of an environmentally sound, energy-efficient future looks like. Nearly everyone leaves impressed.

Ultimately, however, the proof of a building's worth is in its occupancy. Does it work properly? Is it comfortable to the occupants? Does it look nice? And in the case of Audubon House, does it meet the environmental goals it set out to accomplish?

As in any building, there have been glitches, some of them owing to the new or even experimental strategies tried at Audubon House. For example, early on, the customized wood conference tables were found to scratch

---

We were always sick in the old building, and by three in the afternoon we were dragging and had to get coffee. Here we don't have to do that. The lighting is better, for one thing. The recycling is working out very well, too. At first, we had to get used to separating envelopes and paper. Now it's second nature. You just do it automatically.

CATHY LYNCH, MAILROOM SUPERVISOR, NATIONAL AUDUBON SOCIETY

---

easily because, to minimize toxins, they were not sealed with a typical wood finish. The problem was easily solved by buying coasters for coffee drinkers and asking employees to treat the tables gently. The occupancy sensors on the lights had an unintended side effect. In certain conference rooms, the sensors could not pick up the movements of people sitting around the conference table, causing the lights to switch off suddenly after the 6-minute cutoff. The results weren't all bad, however—long, tedious meetings get a brief, humorous recess when the person sitting nearest the sensor does the "wave" to reactivate the lights. Most of the problems at Audubon House, like these, have been small. In contrast, by any measure, the comfort level of employees and the overall performance of the building have been high. Light levels have been found to be satisfactory except in a few isolated cases. The indoor climate has remained at stable, comfortable levels through four seasons, including an exceedingly hot summer. On the subjective scale of "freshness," at least, the quality of the indoor air seemed excellent. Employees spoke positively about pleasant working conditions and spacious layouts, and appeared to be overwhelmingly pleased to be working in the new building.

It's been great here from the first day. There was no chemical smell in the carpet. The ventilation system has been great. I think this is the first time in my work life that I've been totally comfortable for a whole winter. I don't feel tired or or have a headache at the end of the day, and I don't need to take a deep sigh of relief when I get into the street. As for the recycling system, I think it's time we 'walked the talk." In this building, it's possible to do so.
WAYNE MONES, DIRECTOR OF PLANNED GIVING,
NATIONAL AUDUBON SOCIETY

Formal analyses have yet to be done, comparing the actual performance of Audubon House to the environmental goals set by the Audubon Team. Preliminary indications were that the monthly energy bills conformed generally to projected numbers, suggesting that Audubon House was meeting its goal of a 62 percent overall energy reduction. A study of the indoor air quality is just beginning, so no concrete data are available. Numbers are also not yet available on the recycling program program, but recycling is already under way for paper and redeemable beverage cans, a significant portion of the overall waste stream.

In at least one area, however, Audubon House has been an unqualified success: in the hearts and minds of the dedicated people who work for the National Audubon Society. Knowing that the workplace is a living embodiment of the ideals for which they came to work at Audubon is a source of pride for each and every Audubon employee. But that pride does not have to be limited to Audubon people. It is available to all who wish to follow the example of Audubon House.

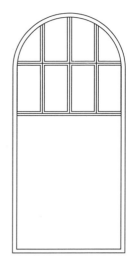

Appendices

Built Environment: Optimization Diagram

APPENDIX

A

This diagram, created by Croxton Collaborative, illustrates the flow of energy and materials through the life of a building project and the associated "upstream" and "downstream" environmental impacts. As can be observed, the building professional's role (center of diagram) in shaping these environmental impacts, while seemingly limited in scope, in actuality determines what and how great the impacts will be through the selection of products, materials, and systems.

How to read the diagram (left to right):

Box 1: Natural resources are extracted, mined, harvested, or collected to manufacture materials and products. Key to resources:
RS = renewable, sustainable
RNS = renewable, nonsustainable
FRE = finite, recyclable
FD = finite, disposable

Box 2: Natural resources are distributed to processing or manufacturing sites.

Box 3: Processing and manufacture of building products and materials. Boxes 1 through 4 together represent the upstream environmental impacts of manufacturing processes.

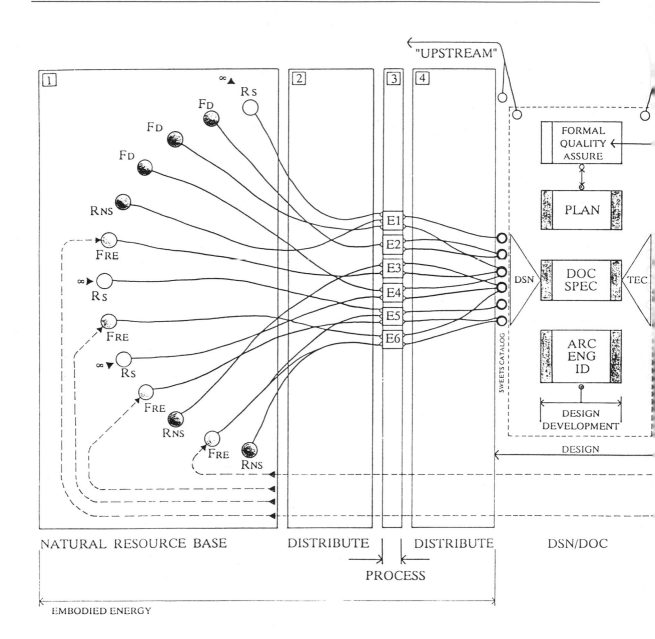

NATURAL RESOURCE BASE

DISTRIBUTE

DISTRIBUTE

DSN/DOC

PROCESS

EMBODIED ENERGY

Rs :Renewable/Sustainable
Rns:Renewable/Non-Sustainable
FR :Finite/Recyclable
FD :Finite/Disposable
EX :Environmental Impact

"DOWNSTREAM"

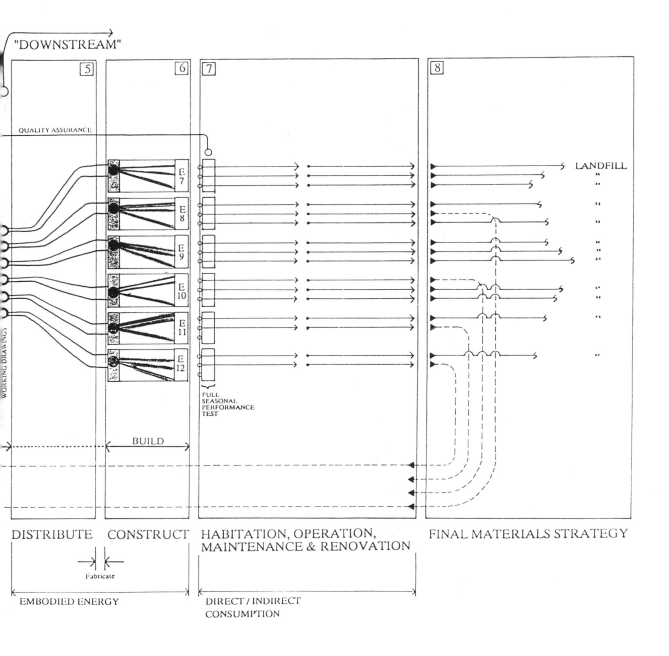

DISTRIBUTE   CONSTRUCT   HABITATION, OPERATION,   FINAL MATERIALS STRATEGY
                         MAINTENANCE & RENOVATION

© *Croxton Collaborative, Architects.*

Box 4: Products and materials are transported from factory to warehouse or distributor.

Center of diagram: Project design—architects, interior designers, and engineers select products and materials, write specifications into the contract documents, which include working drawings of the building.

Box 5: Products and materials distributed for fabrication and/or to the building site for construction.

Box 6: Construction. Boxes 5 through 8 together represent downstream environmental impacts of construction.

Box 7: Habitation, operation, maintenance, and renovation of building. Downstream environmental impacts continue.

Box 8: Used materials and products are disposed of (probably in landfills) or recycled.

Arrows at the bottom of the diagram represent the accumulation of embodied energy in building products and materials up to the habitation phase, and the indirect and direct consumption of energy during habitation.

The DOE-2 Computer Software Program

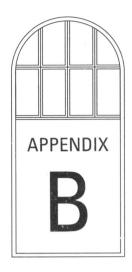

DOE-2 is a computer software program developed by the U.S. Department of Energy and the Electric Power Research Institute in San Francisco, California. The program analyzes the energy performance of a building, hour by hour, throughout the course of a year, taking into consideration geographical location, temperatures, the building's position on the property, dimensions and locations of shaded surfaces, such as overhangs caused by eaves, shadows cast by surrounding buildings, types of materials used in floors, walls, roofing, and windows, and so on.

From this information the program can then measure the life-cycle cost of the building, and various design, material, and building methods can be compared. Four subprograms provide specific information in the following areas.

1. *Systems:* The systems subprogram simulates the operation of secondary HVAC distribution systems, taking into account outside air requirements, operational and control schedules of the building, and the responses of the building materials over time.
2. *Loads:* This part of the program includes formulas recommended by the American Society of Heating, Refrigerating, and Air-Conditioning Engineers used

to calculate hourly heating and cooling loads up to 64 different thermal zones within a building.

3. *Plant:* This aspect of the program simulates operation of the primary HVAC systems, that is, the central heating or cooling plant.

4. *Economics:* It is possible to calculate the cost of energy and the life-cycle cost of the building by considering variables such as fuel and equipment used, the operation of the equipment, and the particulars of local utility rates.

Without this information there can be a tendency to overdesign the building, resulting in higher up-front costs and higher ongoing energy costs.

Local utilities are starting to use this service to evaluate the potential savings of different kinds of designs and materials. Based on information learned from using the DOE-2, some utilities have instituted rebate programs, the savings from the use of a more efficient design to be rebated to a customer over a number of years.

To obtain information about the use of DOE-2 or other building assessment computer programs, contact your local utility to see if it offers the program as a service, or call the Electric Power Research Institute, which is funded by local utilities throughout the country for the purpose of finding cost-saving energy alternatives. The number is 510-855-2183.

Material Safety Data Sheet

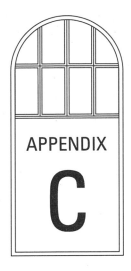

Every manufacturer of a building material is required by law to provide customers with a Material Safety Data Sheet, or MSDS. Below is an an unidentified sample. Following standards set by OSHA (Occupational Safety and Health Administration), the sheet lists percentages and names of hazardous materials that are components of a product. However, it should be noted that very small or "trace" amounts of chemicals and toxins are not required to be reported in these component breakdowns.

From these sheets the team of architect, interior designer, environmental consultant, and owner can make the decision to use the product or reject it for another that may have fewer hazardous materials among its components. It is always better to make a decision after several comparisons of products have been made.

Material Safety Data Sheet

May be used to comply with
OSHA's Hazard Communication Standard,
29 CFR 1910.1200. Standard must be
consulted for specific requirements.

U.S. Department of Labor

Occupational Safety and Health Administration
(Non-Mandatory Form)
Form Approved
OMB No. 1218-0072

NCFR-040489

IDENTITY (As Used on Label and List)
HOMASOTE BOARD* RECYCLED PAPER(CELLULOSE) FIBER

Note: Blank spaces are not permitted. If any item is not applicable, or no information is available, the space must be marked to indicate that.

Section I   * NCFR .

Manufacturer's Name HOMASOTE COMPANY	Emergency Telephone Number 609-883-3300
Address (Number, Street, City, State, and ZIP Code) P.O. BOX 7240	Telephone Number for Information Same as above
W. TRENTON, N.J. 08628	Date Prepared April 4, 1989
(OFF LOWER FERRY ROAD)	Signature of Preparer (optional)

Section II — Hazardous Ingredients/Identity Information

Hazardous Components (Specific Chemical Identity; Common Name(s))	OSHA PEL	ACGIH TLV	Other Limits Recommended	% (optional)
PARAFIN WAX CAS #8002-74-2		$2mg/m^3$		1 to 2
THE FOLLOWING COMPONENTS MAY BE SUBJECT TO ANNUAL REPORTING. SEE SECTION 313 OF				
TITLE III OF SARA.				
ALUMINUM OXIDE CAS #1344-28-1				40% -50%
COPPER COMPOUNDS				LESS THAN 0.1%
NICKLE CAS#7440-02-0				0.15%

Section III — Physical/Chemical Characteristics

Boiling Point	NA	Specific Gravity (H₂O = 1)	0.3-0.6
Vapor Pressure (mm Hg.)	NA	Melting Point	NA
Vapor Density (AIR = 1)	NA	Evaporation Rate (Butyl Acetate = 1)	NA

Solubility in Water

Appearance and Odor
A grey board comprised of interlocking paper fibers, odor - none of slightly aromatic

Section IV — Fire and Explosion Hazard Data

Flash Point (Method Used) NA	Flammable Limits NA	LEL NA	UEL NA

Extinguishing Media
WATER, CO₂, SAND

Special Fire Fighting Procedures
SELF CONTAINED BREATHING APPARATUS RECOMMENDED.

Unusual Fire and Explosion Hazards DEPENDING ON MOISTURE CONTENT, AND PARTICLE DIAMETER, DUST MAY
EXPLODE. AN AIRBORNE CONCENTRATION OF 40 GRAMS OF DUST PER CUBIC METER OF AIR IS
OFTEN USED AS THE LEL FOR CELLULOSIC DUSTS.

(Reproduce locally)

OSHA 174, Sept. 1985

Section V — Reactivity Data

Stability	Unstable		Conditions to Avoid
	Stable	X	

Incompatibility (*Materials to Avoid*)
AVOID OPEN FLAME. PRODUCT MAY IGNITE AT TEMPERATURES IN EXCESS OF 450 F.

Hazardous Decomposition or Byproducts THERMAL-OXIDATIVE DEGRADATION PRODUCES IRRITATING &
TOXIC FUMES AND GASES INCLUDING CO AND CO_2.

Hazardous Polymerization	May Occur		Conditions to Avoid
	Will Not Occur	X	

Section VI — Health Hazard Data

Route(s) of Entry:	Inhalation? YES	Skin? NO	Ingestion? NO

Health Hazards (*Acute and Chronic*)
IRRITATION & OBSTRUCTION DUST CAN CAUSE EYE IRRITATION & INHALATION OF DUST MAY

CAUSE NASAL DRYNESS IF DUST IS NOT PROPERLY CONTROLLED PER OSHA REGULATION 29 CFR,

PART 1910 FOR CELLULOSE AND PARTICULATES.

Carcinogenicity: NA	NTP? NA	IARC Monographs? NA	OSHA Regulated?

Signs and Symptoms of Exposure
IRRITATION

Medical Conditions Generally Aggravated by Exposure DUST MAY CAUSE EYE IRRITATION, NASAL DRYNESS & OBSTRUCTIONS.

Emergency and First Aid Procedures IF IN EYES - TREAT AS A FOREIGN OBJECT; IF RASH OR PERSISTANT
IRRITATION OCCUR GET MEDICAL ADVICE; IF INHALATION OCCURS REMOVE TO FRESH AIR;
IF PERSISTANT COUGHING OR DIFFICULT BREATHING OCCUR GET MEDICAL ADVICE.

Section VII — Precautions for Safe Handling and Use

Steps to Be Taken in Case Material Is Released or Spilled
NA

Waste Disposal Method
DISPOSE OF IN ACCORDANCE WITH LOCAL, COUNTY, STATE & FEDERAL

REGULATIONS.

Precautions to Be Taken in Handling and Storing
NO SPECIAL HANDLING PRECAUTIONS ARE REQUIRED.

Other Precautions
SEE SECTIONS VI & VII IN REGARDS TO DUST.

Section VIII — Control Measures

Respiratory Protection (*Specify Type*)
WEAR A RESPIRATOR APPROVED BY NIOSH IF DUST CONDITIONS EXCEED OSHA RULES & REGULATIONS.

Ventilation	Local Exhaust RECOMMENDED FOR SANDING SAWING & OTHER MACHINING.	Special NA
	Mechanical (*General*) RECOMMENDED AT THE SOURCE OF ANY MECHANICAL CUTTING.	Other NA

Protective Gloves	Eye Protection RECOMMENDED FOR SANDING, SAWING AND OTHER MACHINING.

Other Protective Clothing or Equipment

Work/Hygienic Practices
NO SPECIAL PRACTICES REQUIRED, FOLLOW NORMAL WORK/HYGENIC PRACTICES.

☆ U.S. Government Printing Office: 1987—181-504/64362

Requesting Detailed Product Information Directly from a Manufacturer

Requests for more detailed information about the components of a building material or product can be made directly to the manufacturer. It is best to ask that this information be provided in writing. Below is a typical request for information (name of product and company have been deleted).

14 September 1993

Mr. John Doe
Technical Director/Environmental Officer
XXX Paint Co., Inc.
00 Main St.
Anytown, USA

Dear Mr. Doe:

We are in receipt of your booklet describing your new line of European paints. The booklet is handsome and informative; however, as an architecture and design firm that pursues better environmental products, we need some more information prior to specifying these paints. The information we require is as follows:

For all types of paint products:

VOC counts
- Biocides (type and quantity)
- Fungicides (type and quantity)
- Crystalline silica (%)
- Presence (or not) of any heavy metals associated with brighter paint colors.

Since your paints come from a European source, this information should be readily available. (European manufacturers generally provide environmental data when requested.)

We appreciate your response with the noted information and look forwared to hearing from you.

Yours sincerely,

Kirsten Childs, ASID
Director of Interior Design
Croxton Collaborative

Here is a response from the manufacturer:

September 17, 1993

Ms. Kirsten Childs, ASID
Director of Interior Design
Croxton Collaborative
1122 Madison Ave.
New York, NY 10028

Dear Ms. Childs:

I am in receipt of your letter requesting additional information on our finishes.

1. VOC counts—Please note that in our Specifier's Manual (copy enclosed) there is a technical section

dealing with each finish. Our VOC counts are indicated in this area for each of our finishes.

2. Biocides—There are no biocides in XXX Paint Co. paint.

3. Fungicides—There are no fungicides in XXX Paint Co. paint.

4. Crystalline silica—This compound is believed to be carcinogenic. It does not exist in our paint. It is present in our putty products and applicators are advised to take special precautions when using it.

5. Heavy metals—XXX Paint Co. finishes are compliant with regulations set forth by the U.S. Consumer Products Safety Commission. No lead or other forbidden heavy metals are used in the formulation of our paints.

For your files I have included with this letter a set of MSDS forms on our products. Should you require additional information or documentation, please contact me at 1-800-000-0000.

Cordially,

John Doe
Technical Director
XXX Paint Co., Inc.

APPENDIX

E

Reviewing Results from Chamber Tests

In researching the components of building and office materials it is possible to obtain from a manufacturer results of chamber tests it has arranged to have done by an independent laboratory. In reviewing these test results, look for anomalies, or unexpected turns in the charted levels. For example, below are sample results from a test of formaldehyde emissions of a line of office materials.

Workstation I: Formaldehyde Air Concentration Versus Time

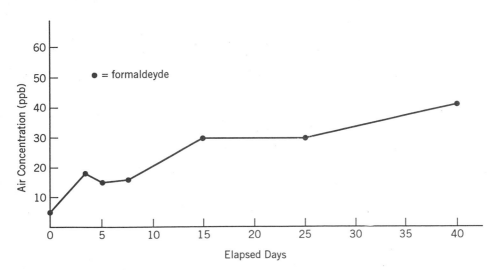

The concentration of formaldehyde is increasing with time; this is a possible reason for alarm, and certainly one requiring further investigation with the vendor.

Workstation II: TVOC Concentration Versus Time

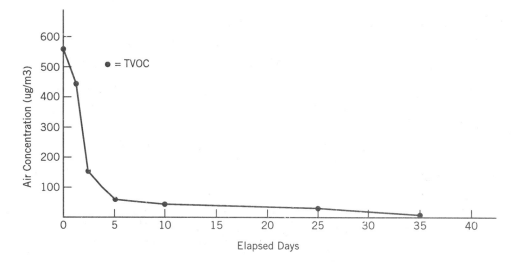

This is a good sign; total volatile organic compounds are decreasing steadily over time.

Carpet: TVOC Emission Rate Versus Time

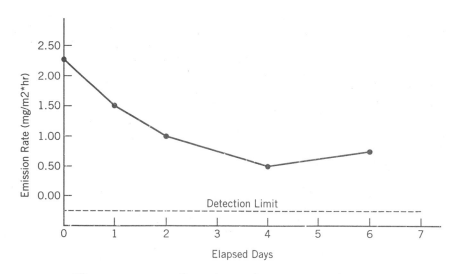

The upturn at day 6 is of concern. The test periods should be extended for further investigation.

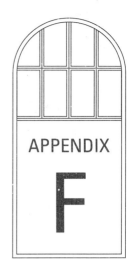

Savings on Lighting

As an example of the possible savings by an energy-efficient lighting system, the graph below shows lighting use at the headquarters of the National Resource Defense Council, in New York City, during the highest-demand month, August, and the lowest-demand month, November. Blips at 3:30 a.m. were caused by the arrival of the cleaning staff. The lines across the top indicate potential use (maximum connected load). The usage has been determined to be less than a quarter of that of a typical office lighting system.

The Green Lights program, developed and sponsored by the U.S. Environmental Protection Agency, will help any company or corporation to upgrade its lighting system with energy-efficient strategies and technology, with the goal of saving money as well as energy. The EPA provides technical support and training, a computer program to analyze and assess retrofit options, and information about financing resources for energy-efficient lighting. For more information, contact: Green Lights, U.S. Environmental Protection Agency, 401 M Street, SW (6202J), Washington, DC 20460; or call 202-775-6650; or FAX 202-775-6680.

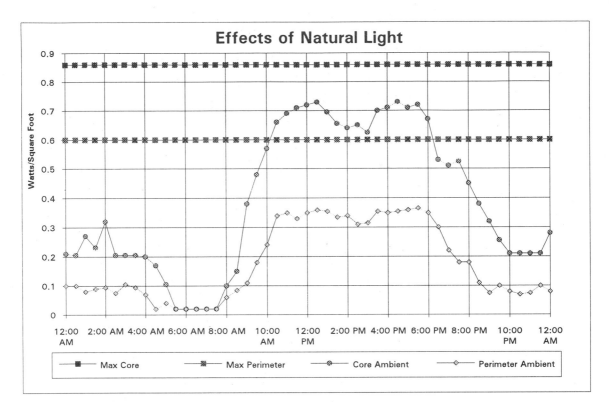

CORE AMBIENT

Time	12:00 AM	2:00 AM	4:00 AM	6:00 AM	8:00 AM	10:00 AM	12:00 PM	2:00 PM	4:00 PM	6:00 PM	8:00 PM	10:00 PM	12:00 AM
W/Sq.	0.21	0.32	0.2	0.02	0.1	0.57	0.72	0.64	0.71	0.67	0.45	0.21	0.28

PERIMETER AMBIENT

Time	12:00 AM	2:00 AM	4:00 AM	6:00 AM	8:00 AM	10:00 AM	12:00 PM	2:00 PM	4:00 PM	6:00 PM	8:00 PM	10:00 PM	12:00 AM
W/Sq.	0.1	0.095	0.07	0.02	0.06	0.24	0.35	0.34	0.35	0.35	0.18	0.08	0.08

Courtesy of Flack + Kurtz.

Resources: Materials, Studies, Guides

To locate a laboratory that can test materials used in building, you may refer to the following book:

International Directory of Testing Laboratories (PCN 32-333293-32) Over 1,400 laboratories are featured, mostly in the United States. $69 prepaid in U.S. and Canada; 7% shipping charge is added if not prepaid.

Call, FAX, or write for this book from: The American Society for Testing and Materials, 1916 Race Street, Philadelphia, PA 19103; Customer Service: 215-299-5585 or FAX 215-977-9679.

ASTM offers a wide range of publications guiding architects, engineers, and builders through the material selection process. ASTM also sells the following guides to assessing the environmental standards of existing buildings:

Practice for Environmental Site Assessment: Phase I Environmental Site Assessment Process (E-15270)
Practice for Environmental Site Assessment: Transaction Screening Process (E-1528)

These guides are $23 each prepaid in U.S. and Canada; 7% shipping charge will be added if not prepaid.

Environmental Resource Guide, jointly produced by the EPA and the American Institute of Architects, is a quarterly subscription service, including analysis of commonly specified building materials, research from EPA labs, as well as articles, case studies, and bibliographies for interested professionals. The cost is $195 per year for AIA members, $225 for nonmembers. For information or to order a subscription, write to AIA Order Department, 9 Jay Gould Court, P.O. Box 753, Waldorf, MD 20604; or call 1-800-365-ARCH(2724).

For the latest studies, newsletters, and directory of agencies and consultants concerning indoor air quality, contact: Indoor Air Quality Publications, 4520 East-West Highway, Suite 610, Bethesda, MD 20814 or call 301-913-0115.

For a catalog of environmentally sustainable building products and materials, contact Environmental Outfitters, 44 Crosby Street, New York, N.Y. 10012, 212-334-9659 or FAX 203-966-2807.

One reliable source for finding wood sources that do not contribute to the destruction of tropical forests is the Rainforest Alliance's "Smart Wood Certification Program." Contact the Rainforest Alliance, 65 Bleecker Street, New York, NY 10012-2420; 212-677-1900, or FAX 212-677-2187.

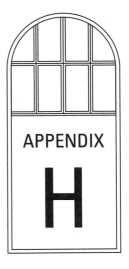

The Audubon Garbage Test

Audubon's seven-day Garbage Test was developed in 1990 as part of the society's Solid Solutions for Solid Waste program. The test is a means for a business, institution, or household to assess its total yearly output of waste as well as the potential for recovery and recycling. In addition, it is an excellent way to teach people about how much waste they generate and the importance of recycling. As such, it can be used to prepare employees for implementation of a recycling program.

To begin the test, select a leader in each department or area of the office to help supervise and guide employees. In each area, place 12 cartons or sturdy trash bags in an easily accessible location for the collection of materials. The bags or boxes should be labeled according to the following categories:

1. Hazardous or other waste that does not get mixed with the general waste stream. *Examples:* white-out, fluorescent tubes, batteries, copier toner, paints, polishes.
2. Newspapers, magazines, glossy brochures (includes material that is now, or soon will be, recyclable into newsprint, but not higher grades of paper). *Examples:* all dry newspapers and magazines.
3. White office and computer (green-bar) paper.
4. Mixed paper. *Examples:* colored office paper; clean, dry paper from take-out restaurants; manila folders;

interoffice envelopes; envelopes without labels; phone books; miscellaneous junk mail.

5. Other paper. *Examples:* Post-its or other sticky paper, soiled take-out cardboard, fax paper, paper with labels.
6. Corrugated cardboard.
7. Compostables. *Examples:* lunch and food waste; soft, wet paper; tissues; coffee grounds.
8. Mixed materials. *Examples:* ball-point and other disposable pens, pencils, paper envelopes with bubble wrap, liners, reports in plastic covers not easily removed, damaged computer disks.
9. Plastics. *Examples:* Styrofoam packing material, wrapping, take-out food containers that have been washed.
10. Glass, cans, metals. *Examples:* clean or washed containers, broken paper clips.
11. Electric or other heavy equipment. *Examples:* broken clock, fan.
12. Anything else.

For one week, have employees sort their waste and discard in the appropriate boxes. At the end of the week (or once a day, if you prefer), weigh the contents of each box or bag. Add the total weight of all categories and divide into the weight of each category to calculate the percentage of each.

Divide the total waste collected by the number of people involved in the test, then by the number of days over which the test was taken. This provides an estimate of how much waste is generated per person per day. Multiply waste per day by the number of working days in a year to determine the total waste per person per year.

Diseminate the results of the test to your employees so they can see their contribution to the office waste stream. Determine which categories of materials are currently recyclable in your location; which are likely to be recyclable; which can easily be eliminated, reduced, or reused; and which will continue to be disposed of as "trash." Use the results to design a realistic recycling and waste reduction program for your office and to set goals for future recycling.

Products Used at Audubon House

The products listed below were chosen by the National Audubon Society and Croxton Collaborative for use in Audubon House. The list is provided for informational value only. The National Audubon Society and Croxton Collaborative do not endorse these or any other products. We take no responsibility for the performance of, or reader satisfaction with, any product listed herein. In addition, the local product market should be researched prior to purchasing from distant locations.

We recommend that you obtain and review manufacturers' current specifications and related information to determine the suitability of any product for your own purposes. Further, please keep in mind that the market for these types of products is changing rapidly. Since the time the Audubon Team made its decisions, the manufacturers below may have modified their products, and other manufacturers may have made new products available. (Specifications for the items listed were completed in January–February 1991.)

The Glidden Company
925 Euclid Avenue
Cleveland, OH 44115
(216) 344-8140

Spred 2000; Lifemaster
2000 paint

Sylvania Lighting   Lamps
100 Endicott Street
Danvers, MA 01923
(508) 777-1900

AirKrete   Insulation
Palmer Industries Inc.
10611 Old Annapolis Road
Frederick, MD 21701
(301) 898-7848

Homasote   Subflooring
Box 7940
West Trenton, NJ 08628
(609) 883-3300/
(516) 628-3626

Desso   Carpeting
P.O. Box 1351
Wayne, PA 19087
(800) 368-1515

Southwall Technologies   Heat-mirror™ windows
1029 Corporation Way
Palo Alto, CA 94303
(415) 962-9111

Herman Miller   Furniture systems
855 East Main Avenue
Zeeland, MI 49464
(616) 654-3316

Dixie Manufacturing Co.   Carpet padding
P.O. Box 59
Norfolk, VA 23501
804-625-8251

Linear Lighting   Pendant fixtures (lighting)
Stan Deutsch Associates
31-30 Hunter's Point
 Avenue
Long Island City, NY 11101
718-361-7552

Zumtobel
141 Lanza Avenue
Garfield, NJ 07026
201-340-8900

Pendant fixtures (lighting)

Lightolier
100 Lighting Way
Secaucus, NJ 07096-1508
201-864-3000

Downlights

Agents with Carcinogenic Risks to Human Beings

The December 1986 Working Group of the International Agency for Research on Cancer has published the following lists of agents believed to be carcinogenic (cancer causing) in human beings and experimental animals. This list can be used to compare relative risks when examining MSDS sheets or other product information provided by a manufacturer.

Group 1. The Working Group concluded that the following agents are carcinogenic to human beings.

Aflatoxins
Aluminum production
4-Aminobiphenyl
Analgesic mixtures containing phenacetin
Arsenic and arsenic compounds*
Asbestos
Auramine, manufacture of
Azathioprine
Benzene
Benzidine
Betel quid with tobacco
N,N-Bis(2-chloroethyl)-2-naphthylamine (chlorna-
    phazine)
Bis(chloromethyl)ether and chloromethyl methyl
    ether (technical grade)

Boot and shoe manufacture and repair
1,4-Butanediol dimethanesulfonate (Myleran)
Chlorambucil
1-(2-Chloroethyl)-3(4-methylcyclohexyl)-1-
  nitrosourea (methyl-CCNU)
Chromium compounds, hexavalent*
Coal gasification
Coal-tar pitches
Coal tars
Coke production
Cyclophosphamide
Diethylstilbestrol
Erionite
Estrogen replacement therapy
Estrogens, nonsteroidal*
Estrogens, steroidal*
Furniture and cabinet making
Hematite mining, underground, with exposure to
  radon
Iron and steel founding
Isopropyl alcohol manufacture, strong-acid process
Magenta, manufacture of
Melphalan
8-Methoxypsoralen (methoxsalen) plus ultraviolet ra-
  diation
Mineral oils, untreated and mildly treated
MOPP (combined therapy with nitrogen mustard, vin-
  cristine, procarbazine, and prednisone) and other
  combined chemotherapy, including alkylating
  agents
Mustard gas (sulfur mustard)
2-Naphthylamine
Nickel and nickel compounds*
Oral contraceptives, combined†
Oral contraceptives, sequential
The rubber industry
Shale oils

---

* This evaluation applies to the group of chemicals as a whole and not necessarily to all individual chemicals within the group.
† There is also conclusive evidence that these agents have a protective effect
against cancers of the ovary and endometrium.

Soots
Talc containing asbestiform fibers
Tobacco products, smokeless
Tobacco smoke
Treosulfan
Vinyl chloride

Group 2A. The Working Group concluded that the following agents are probably carcinogenic to human beings.

Acrylonitrile
Adriamycin
Androgenic (anabolic) steroids
Benz[a]anthracene
Benzidine-based dyes
Benzzo[*a*]pyrene
Beryllium and beryllium compounds
Bischloroethyl nitrosourea (BCNU)
Cadmium and cadmium compounds
1-(2-Chloroethyl)-3-cyclohexyl-1-nitrosourea (CCNU)
Cisplatin
Creosotes
Dibenz[*a,h*]anthracene
Diethyl sulphate
Dimethylcarbamoyl chloride
Dimethyl sulfate
Epichlorohydrin
Ethylene dibromide
Ethylene oxide
N-Ethyl-*N*-nitrosourea
Formaldehyde
5-Methoxypsoralen
4,4′-Methylene bis(2-chloroaniline) (MOCA)
N-Methyl-*N*′-nitro-*N*-nitrosoguanidine (MNNG)
N-Methyl-*N*-nitrosourea
Nitrogen mustard
N-Nitrosodiethylamine
N-Nitrosodimethylamine
Phenacetin
Polychlorinated biphenyls (PCBs)
Procarbazine hydrochloride

Propylene oxide
Styrene oxide
Tris(1-aziridinyl)phosphine sulfide (Thio-TEPA)
Tris(2,3-dibromopropyl) phosphate
Vinyl bromide

Group 2B. The Working Group concluded that the following agents are possibly carcinogenic to human beings.

A-α-C (2-Amino-9H-pyrido[2,3-b]indole)
Acetaldehyde
Acetamide
Acrylamide
AF-2 [2-(2-Furyl)-3(5-nitro-2-furyl)acrylamide]
para-Aminoazobenzene
ortho-Aminoazotoluene
2-Amino-5-(5-nitro-2-furyl)-1,3,4-thiadiazole
Amitrole
ortho-Anisidine
Aramite®
Auramine, technical grade
Azaserine
Benzo[b]fluoranthene
Benzo[j]fluoranthene
Benzo[k]fluoranthene
Benzyl violet 4B
Bitumens, extracts of steam refined and air refined
Bleomycins
Bracken fern
1,3-Butadiene
Butylated hydroxyanisole (BHA)
β-Butyrolactone
Carbon-black extracts
Carbon tetrachloride
Carpentry and joinery
Carrageenan, degraded
Chloramphenicol
Chlordecone (Kepone)
α-Chlorinated toluenes
Chloroform
Chlorophenols

Chlorophenoxy herbicides
4-Chloro-*ortho*-phenylenediamine
para-Chloro-*ortho*-toluidine
Citrus Red No. 2
para-Cresidine
Cycasin
Dacarbazine
Daunomycin
DDT
N,N'-Diacetylbenzidine
2,4-Diaminoanisole
4,4'-Diaminodiphenyl ether
2,4-Diaminotoluene
Dibenz[*a,h*]acridine
Dibenz[*a,i*]acridine
7*H*-Dibenzo[*c,g*]carbazole
Dibenzo[*a,e*]pyrene
Dibenzo[*a,h*]pyrene
Dibenzo[*a,i*]pyrene
Dibenzo[*a,l*]pyrene
1,2-Dibromo-3-chloropropane
para-Dichlorobenzene
3,3'-Dichlorobenzidine
3,3'-Dichloro-4,4'-diaminodiphenyl ether
1,2-Dichloroethane
Dichloromethane
1,3-Dichloropropene (technical grade)
Diepoxybutane
Di(2-ethylhexyl)phthalate
1,2-Diethylhydrazine
Diglycidyl resorcinol ether
Dihydrosafrole
3,3'-Dimethoxybenzidine (*ortho*-dianisidine)
para-Dimethylaminoazobenzene
trans-2-[(Dimethylamino)methylimino]-5-[2-(5-
    nitro-2-furyl)vinyl]1,3,4-oxadiazole
3,3'-Dimethylbenzidine (*ortho*-tolidine)
1,1-Dimethylhydrazine
1,2-Dimethylhydrazine
1,4-Dioxane
Ethyl acrylate

Ethylene thiourea

Ethyl methanesulfonate 2-(2-Formylhydrazino)-4-(5-nitro-2-furyl)thiazole

Glu-P-1 (2-Amino-6-methyldipyrido[1,2-*a*:3',2'-*d*]imidazole)

Glu-P-2 (2-Aminodipyrido[1,2-*a*:3'2'-*d*]imidazole)

Glycidaldehyde

Griseofulvin

Hexachlorobenzene

Hexachlorocyclohexanes

Hexamethylphosphoramide

Hydrazine

Indeno[1,2,3-*cd*]pyrene

IQ (2-Amino-3-methylimidazo[4,5-*f*]quinoline)

Iron-dextran complex

Lasiocarpine

Lead and lead compounds, inorganic

MeA-α-C (2-Amino-3-methyl-9*H*-pyrido[2,3-*b*]indole)

Medroxyprogesterone acetate

Merphalan

2-Methylaziridine

Methylazoxymethanol and its acetate

5-Methylchrysene

4,4'-Methylene bis(2-methylaniline)

4,4'-Methylenedianiline

Methyl methanesulfonate

2-Methyl-1-nitroanthraquinone (uncertain purity)

N-Methyl-*N*-nitrosourethane

Methylthiouracil

Metronidazole

Mirex

Mitomycin C

Monocrotaline

5-(Morpholinomethyl)-3-[(5-nitrofurfurylidene)amino]-2-oxazolidinone

Nafenopin

Niridazole

5-Nitroacenaphthene

Nitrofen (technical grade)

1-[(5-Nitrofurfurylidene)amino]-2-imidazolidinone

N-[4-(5-Nitro-2-furyl)-2-thiazolyl]acetamide

Nitrogen mustard *N*-oxide
2-Nitropropane
N-Nitrosodi-*n*-butylamine
N-Nitrosodiethanolamine
N-Nitrosodi-*n*-propylamine
3-(*N*-Nitrosomethylamino)propionitrile
4-(*N*-Nitrosomethylamino)-1-(3-pyridyl-1-butanone
   (NNK)
N-Nitrosomethylethylamine
N-Nitrosomethylvinylamine
N-Nitrosomorpholine
N'-Nitrosonornicotine
N-Nitrosopiperidine
N-Nitrosopyrrolidine
N-Nitrososarcosine
Oil Orange SS
Panfuran S (containing dihydroxymethylfuratrizine)
Phenazopyridine hydrochloride
Phenobarbital
Phenoxybenzamine hydrochloride
Phenytoin
Polybrominated biphenyls
Ponceau MX
Ponceau 3R
Potassium bromate
Progestins
1,3-Propane sultone
B-Propiolactone
Propylthiouracil
Saccharin
Safrole
Sodium *ortho*-phenylphenate
Sterigmatocystin
Streptozotocin
Styrene
Sulfallate
2,3,7,8-Tetrachlorodibenzo-*para*-dioxin (TCDD)
Tetrachloroethylene
Thioacetamide
4,4'-Thiodianiline
Thiourea

Toluene diisocyanates
ortho-Toluidine
Toxaphene (polychlorinated camphenes)
Trp-P-1 (3-Amino-1,4-dimethyl-5*H*-pyrido[4,3-*b*]
  indole)
Trp-P-2 (3-Amino-1-methyl-5*H*-pyrido[4,3-*b*]indole)
Trypan blue
Uracil mustard
Urethane

Suppliers of Absorption Chiller-Heater Equipment

The vendors listed below manufacture or sell absorption chiller-heater equipment such as that used at Audubon House. This list is provided for informational value only. The National Audubon Society and Croxton Collaborative do not endorse any of these manufacturers or suppliers. We are not responsible for the performance of, or reader satisfaction with, these products.

Please keep in mind that the market for such equipment is changing rapidly. Since the time Audubon made its decisions, the manufacturers and suppliers listed below may have modified their products or new products may have come on the market. We recommend that you obtain and review manufacturers' current specifications and related information to determine the suitability of the equipment to your purposes. Bear in mind also that location, climate conditions, available fuel sources, and other factors should also be considered in determining selection of system(s).

American Yazaki Corp.
13740 Omega Road
Farmers Branch, TX
75244
(214) 385-8725

The Carrier Corp.
P.O. Box 4808
Syracuse, NY 13221
(315) 432-6000

McQuay, A Division of
Snyder General Corp.
13600 Industrial Park
Blvd.
Minneapolis, MN 55441
(612) 553-5366

The Robur Corp.
2300 Lynch Road, P.O.
Box 3792
Evansville, IN 47736-3792
(812) 424-1800

The Trane Co.
3600 Pammel Creek Road
La Crosse, WI 54601
(608) 787-2000

York International Corp.
P.O. Box 1592
York, PA 17405-1592
(717) 771-6355

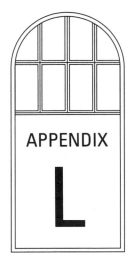

APPENDIX

L

Glossary

Ambient Lighting. Ambient light is room area light or outdoor light incident to a location at the time of measurement or operations. It may come from direct or indirect fixtures and from windows and/or skylights. It is usually not directed to a specific work area or object.

Biological Contamination. Biological contamination of building environments is caused by bacteria, molds and their spores, pollen, viruses, and other biological material. It is often linked to poorly designed and maintained HVAC systems. Biological contaminants may breed in stagnant water allowed to accumulate in humidifiers and cooling coil condensate pans, or where water has collected on ceiling tiles, carpeting, insulation, and internally lined ductwork. People exposed to a biologically contaminated environment may display physical symptoms that include cough, tightness in the chest, fever, chills, muscle aches, and general allergic-type responses such as mucous membrane irritation and upper respiratory congestion.

Building-Related Illness. A clinically defined sickness, disease, or infirmity resulting from occupant exposure to indoor pollutants. People exposed to the environment of a building that manifests BRI may display symptoms ranging from cough, fever, and chills to serious respiratory illness and damage to liver and kidneys. Complaints of BRI may require extended recovery time after affected persons leave the building.

CFCs. Chlorofluorocarbons, a family of organic chemical compounds. They are used as propellants in pressurized aerosol cans (now banned), as heat exchange fluids in refrigerators, freezers, and air conditioners, and as mold release and blowing agents in industry. They are also found in cleaning fluids. Released into the air, CFCs migrate into the stratosphere, where they are broken down by ultraviolet light into reactive fragments that destroy ozone. In addition to stratospheric ozone depletion, CFCs that are released into the atmosphere contribute to **global warming.** Global warming is caused by the greenhouse effect of certain gases that trap the earth's heat. For this reason, CFCs are considered **greenhouse gases.** Another greenhouse gas is carbon dioxide, the greatest contributor to global warming.

Coefficient of Performance. A value used in relation to heat pumps or refrigeration machines. It is the ratio of the amount of heat delivered to the energy input to the machine. Thus C.O.P. = energy output/energy input.

Downstream Impacts. Impacts to the environment that are caused by consumer use and disposal of products. In the case of construction, downstream impacts include those resulting from site preparation, demolition of existing structures and/or materials, and general construction waste materials. Significantly, downstream waste can be mitigated directly by separating materials and recycling all those for which recycling centers exist.

Embodied Energy. The energy consumed in the construction of a building. It includes the energy used by construction machinery and the energy required to obtain, process, and transport raw materials used for construction. The embodied energy concept is a vital one for understanding the loss incurred when buildings are demolished rather than recycled.

Footcandle. A unit of illumination. Illumination is a measure of the number of lumens falling on each square foot of a surface. One footcandle is the amount of direct light emitted by one candela that falls on one square foot of a surface on which every point is one foot away from the source. If a light of 80 lumens is falling uniformly on a table of 4 feet squared, the illumination of that table is 20 lumens per square foot, or 20 footcandles.

HVAC System. Heating, ventilation, and air-conditioning system in a building. The HVAC system controls the environment of a building.

Indoor Air Quality (Acceptable). ASHRAE defines this as air in which there are no known contaminants at harmful concentrations as determined by cognizant authorities and with which a substantial majority (80 percent or more) of the people exposed do not express dissatisfaction.

Life Cycle. The original source, transportation, processing, use, and final disposal or secondary (recycled) use of a product.

Load-Bearing Wall. In a structure, a wall that bears weight. Acting like a continuous column, a load-bearing wall transfers a dead weight vertically to the ground. In this way it is unlike a partition wall, which does not take load but does separate two spaces (although a partition wall may also be load bearing).

Postconsumer Waste. Wastes from products that have passed through the hands of end users (consumers). Examples include newspapers, magazines, beverage containers, building materials, and so on. Postconsumer waste makes up the bulk of what goes to landfills, is incinerated, or is otherwise disposed of, absent recycling programs.

Preconsumer Waste. Waste that is generated before a product has reached its end user. Examples include unprinted and printed paper scraps generated by paper mills, converters, printers, and publishers, glass scraps from light-bulb manufacture, and so on. Although recycling of preconsumer waste is important, it is widely thought that it is insufficient to deal with the problem of solid waste disposal.

***R*-Value.** A measure of the thermal resistance of a material. Thermal resistance is the opposition of material and air spaces to the flow of heat by conduction, convection, and radiation.

Sick Building Syndrome. Health problems associated with working in "sick" building environments. Indoor air problems cited as contributing factors to sick buildings include inadequate ventilation, pollutant emissions within the building, contamination from outside sources, and biological contamination. Symptoms include acute discomfort in the form of headache; eye, nose, or throat irritation; dry cough; dry, itchy skin; dizziness and nausea; difficulty in concentrating; fatigue; and sensitivity to odors. A building is probably sick if a significant number of occupants show SBS symptoms, the cause of the symptoms is unknown, and most occupants report relief upon leaving the building.

Task Lighting. Any form of light that is focused on a specific surface or object. It is intended to provide high-quality lighting (often flexible) for a predetermined activity such as writing, reading, working with special equipment, or using a computer terminal.

Thermal Envelope. The outside shell of a building. It acts as a barrier between the environment inside a building and that outside a building. Essentially, the thermal envelope consists of the exterior walls and windows, and the roof and skylights.

Upstream Impacts. Those impacts to the environment that are caused by the extraction of raw materials, transportation, and the manufacturing process of products used in construction. Control over upstream impacts can be exercised by the choice of products, which may be formalized in purchasing guidelines.

VOCs. Volatile organic compounds, chemicals that contain carbon molecules and that are volatile enough to evaporate from material surfaces into indoor air at normal temperatures. (This occurrence is called off-gassing.) VOCs such as formaldehyde are found in many materials used in the typical office building. Solvents, paints, adhesives, carpeting, rubber molding, particle-board, photocopiers, and cleaning agents are likely sources of VOC emissions. Prolonged exposure to VOCs can lead to acute, chronic health problems. Some VOCs are known carcinogens.

Index

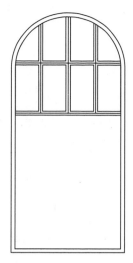

The National Audubon Society invites you to contribute to its work toward conservation and restoration of natural ecosystems, which includes the promotion of environmentally responsible design.

To become a member call: 1-800-274-4201

For more information write: National Audubon Society
Conservation Information
700 Broadway
New York, NY 10003